SAVING ME FIRST
I

SAVING ME FIRST
I

A QUEST FOR THE TRUE SELF

STORY BY HUI BEOP
ART BY JULIE KIM

THE PRACTITIONER'S EDITION

Text Copyright © 2018 by Hui Beop
Illustration Copyright © 2018 by Julie Kim

All rights reserved. This book or any portion thereof may not be reproduced or used in any manner whatsoever without the express written permission of the publisher except for the use of brief quotations in a book review.

The content of this book is designed to provide entertainment as well as helpful information to the reader. This book is not meant to be used, nor should it be used to diagnose or treat any medical condition. For diagnosis or treatment of medical problems and conditions, consult with your own physician/practitioners. The author and publisher are not liable for any physical, psychological, emotional, financial, or commercial damages, including, but not limited to, special, incidental, consequential or other damages. You are responsible for your own choices, actions, and results.

Text Font: Mighty Zeo Caps 2.0

Printed in the United States of America

Practitioner's Edition, 2018

ISBN 978-0-9998771-1-1 (hardback)
ISBN 978-0-9998771-9-7 (paperback)
ISBN 978-0-9998771-5-9 (ebook)

www.savingmefirst.com

SAVING ME FIRST

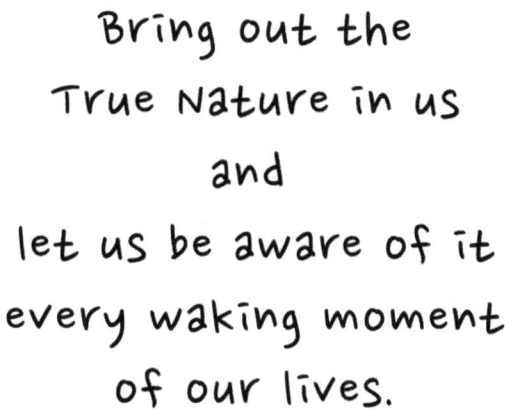

Bring out the
True Nature in us
and
let us be aware of it
every waking moment
of our lives.

CONTENTS

PART 1: LOST

THE WAKE-UP CALL 3

ASK THE DOCTORS 9

NEW REALITY: COMPASSION FOR THE BODY 15

MEDITATION 19

LOST 21

THE CELESTIAL VISIT..23

THE LOGICAL MIND 1 27

THE LOGICAL MIND 2 30

THE WISE DOCTOR 34

THE LECTURE 36

THE CROWS 39

THE PHONE CALL TO THE ZEN MASTER 45

MEETING THE ZEN MASTER 51

SELLING OFF ALL 60

FINALLY AT THE SAN FRANCISCO ZEN CENTER 61

PART 2: TO RECOVERY

NEW LIFE 69

THE UNHOLY ZEN MASTER 70

THE HERB PANTRY 72

FIVE ORGANS AND THEIR FUNCTION 76

THE WISE COUNTRY DOCTOR 78

REFLECT AND REPENT/SELF-KNOWING 83

THE HEAD-SHAVING CEREMONY 87

SUTRA 88

EATING OUT WITH THE ZEN MASTER 92

"+" AND "-" EQUALS HARMONY 98

SHEDDING 54 POUNDS 111

FUNCTIONS 116

MENDING OLD WOUNDS 120

THE ZEN MASTER WHO SWEPT AND POLISHED 123

KOAN 1 128

KOAN 2 128

KOAN 3 130

SEE YOURSELF THROUGH OTHERS! 131

GOLDEN GATE BRIDGE 134

THE BLOOD SERMON - STARS AND BRUISES 137

THE ENERGIES AT BIRTH 142

BEING CONNECTED 147

TWENTY-ONE DAYS TO HONOR HER PARENTS 150

LEAVING SAN FRANCISCO - A NECESSARY
DEPARTURE 157

PART 3: RECLAIMED

MEETING MOTHER ZEN MASTER 163

THE ZEN WORLD - THE FIRST VISIT 169

        THE SECOND VISIT 172

        THE THIRD VISIT 174

        THE FOURTH VISIT......................176

THE DEPARTURE 180

MOUNT JIRI TRAINING CENTER 182

FINDING ROOTS 194

THE RETURN 195

THE ORDINATION PROCESSION 196

THE ORDINATION AND REGISTRATION 198

THE GREAT GRAND MASTERS' INSTRUCTIONS 201

OPENING OF THE DRAGON'S EYES 204

THE FIRST ENERGY PORTAL
EARTHLY ARRIVAL

ONCE UPON A TIME, A PECULIAR LITTLE GIRL ENTERED THIS EARTHLY LIFE, UNPREPARED FOR ALL THE SUFFERING THAT "LIVING" ENTAILED.

HER AGELESS SOUL, DESPERATE TO RETURN TO HER PLACE OF ORIGIN, LOOKED FOR AN ENLIGHTENED BEING WHO COULD GUIDE HER BACK HOME. SHE WAITED AND WAITED FOR THAT WISE PERSON TO RESCUE HER FROM THIS WORLD OF PAIN AND CONFUSION, BUT NO ONE CAME.

INSTEAD, THE LITTLE GIRL WAS EDUCATED AND GROOMED TO BE A PROPER YOUNG LADY SO SHE COULD FIND A GOOD HUSBAND AND LIVE "HAPPILY EVER AFTER". OF COURSE, FOR THE LITTLE GIRL, THAT WAS NO "HAPPILY EVER AFTER". HER HAPPINESS WOULD BE IN ESCAPING THIS CHAOTIC WORLD AND RETURNING HOME.

WHEN SHE TOLD EVERYONE WHAT SHE TRULY WANTED, EVERYONE THOUGHT THAT HER IDEAS WERE STRANGE, WITH THE EXCEPTION OF HER FATHER. HE SEEMED TO UNDERSTAND HER ANGUISH AND HER DESIRE TO RETURN, BUT HE WAS POWERLESS TO HELP HER. THE REST OF THE PEOPLE ADMONISHED HER TO GO ALONG AND DO AS EVERYONE ELSE DOES. THEY SAID IT WOULD BE THE ONLY WAY SHE'D FIT IN AND FIND ANY SUPPORT FROM THOSE AROUND HER, BE IT FAMILY, FRIENDS AND STRANGERS.

So, the little girl grew up to become a worldly young woman. She lived as others lived, tasting the sweet and bitter fruits of life. She experienced pain, addiction, likes and dislikes, and occasionally, joy.

And the support that was promised her was not real, she later learned. It was usually the conditional kind that would be given only if she followed the rules and desires of the one giving the support. She clung to this false support nevertheless because she had no other options before her.

Profoundly alone and empty, the now young woman looked around for a role to play. There was the good wife and the successful professional. Perhaps she should follow the money, since it seemed to be the key to everything in this world.

And so the little girl, in her womanhood, lived her life like everyone else. Though it was aimless, it wasn't a bad life. She had the material trappings of success as well as recognition for all her accomplishments. It looked as if she would be spending the rest of her life this way. Eventually, she forgot that she was adrift and far away from where she needed to be.

That is, until she received a wake-up call from her place of origin. It was time to come home.

PART I
LOST

THE WAKE-UP CALL

CONNEE, 35 YEARS OLD 5-FOOT-6 AND 125 POUNDS, WORKS IN THE CREDIT DEPARTMENT OF THE LOCAL NEWSPAPER COMPANY. SHE HAS NO CHILDREN AND IS FINANCIALLY STABLE.

SHE IS GOOD AT WHAT SHE DOES.
SHE IS FIERCELY INDEPENDENT AND CONFIDENT.
A DIVORCEE, SHE LIVES ALONE.
SHE HAS A LARGE CIRCLE OF FRIENDS, BUT SHE IS CLOSEST TO JACK.
EVERYTHING SHE SETS HER MIND TO, SHE ACCOMPLISHES AND RECEIVES.
SHE STRIVES TO BE THE BEST SHE CAN BE AT ANY GIVEN TIME—EVEN BOWLING A 300 AND GOLFING A HOLE IN ONE.
AND CONNEE HAS EVERY REASON TO BELIEVE THAT THIS TRAJECTORY WILL CONTINUE.

ONE FALL, CONNEE WENT TO WORK AND FOUND THAT HER BODY SUDDENLY CEASED TO FUNCTION THE WAY IT USED TO.

I CAN'T LIFT MY HEAD...

NEITHER HER BODY NOR HER MIND WAS FUNCTIONING LIKE NORMAL. AFTER TAKING A FEW HOURS OF REST ON THE LADIES LOUNGE SOFA, CONNEE TRIED TO GET HER BODY TO RETURN TO WORK. HOWEVER, HER CONDITION WORSENED.

HER BODY FELT LIKE IT WAS FALLING APART. CONNEE REALIZED THAT SHE WAS DONE FOR THE DAY.

I THINK I'M SICK. I NEED TO GO HOME.

I NOTICED THAT. CAN YOU DRIVE?

THE MANAGER OFFERED TO DRIVE HER HOME, BUT CONNEE ASSURED HER THAT SHE WAS OKAY TO DRIVE. CONNEE DIDN'T FULLY UNDERSTAND THE SERIOUSNESS OF HER CONDITION.

AFTER GETTING HER STUFF TOGETHER, SHE SLOWLY MADE HER WAY TO THE CAR.

YOU HAVE GOT TO WAKE UP AND GET HOME.

HER ATTENTION SPAN LASTED ONLY TWO MINUTES AT A TIME.

UGH. YOU CANNOT GIVE OUT ON ME...

SLIPPING IN AND OUT OF CONSCIOUSNESS AS SHE DROVE SLOWLY HOME, CONNEE HEARD THE BLARE OF A POLICE SIREN FROM BEHIND. SHE PULLED OVER TO THE SHOULDER AND PARKED HER CAR.

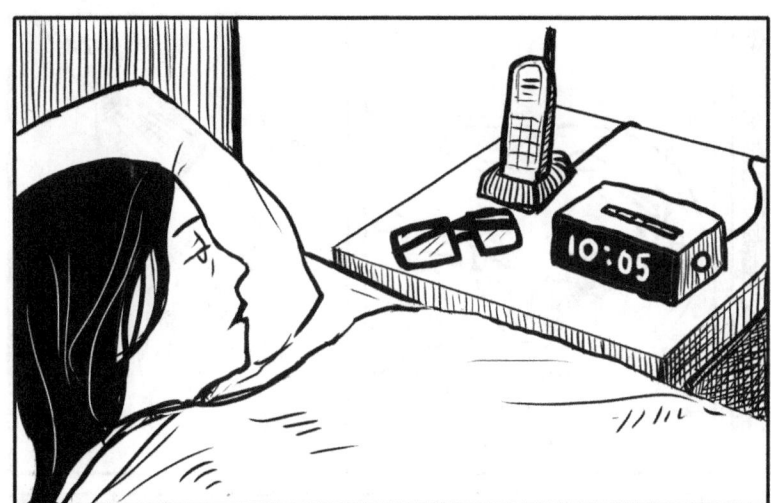

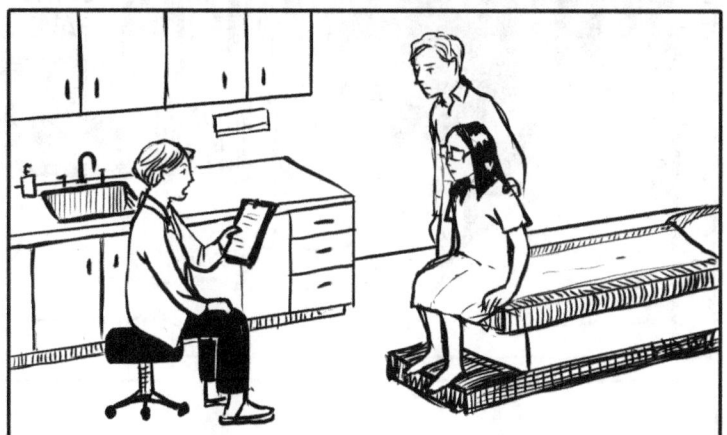

CONNEE WAS MOSTLY CONFINED TO THE BED. SHE HAD TO TAKE A LEAVE OF ABSENCE FROM WORK.

JACK CAME REGULARLY TO CHECK UP ON CONNEE.

COOKING AND CLEANING THE HOUSE WAS IMPOSSIBLE FOR HER.

SO WAS TAKING A NICE HOT SHOWER.

SHE COULDN'T CARRY ON A CONVERSATION AS SHE SLIPPED IN AND OUT OF CONSCIOUSNESS.

WHO WAS I TRYING TO CALL?

HER INDOMITABLE WILL HAD LEFT HER.

IN ITS PLACE WAS EXCRUCIATING PAIN THAT BURNED THROUGH EVERY PART OF HER BODY.

SHE WOKE UP THE NEXT DAY.

CONNEE HAD TWO SPOONFULS OF SOUP.
THAT WAS THE ONLY AMOUNT SHE COULD TAKE.

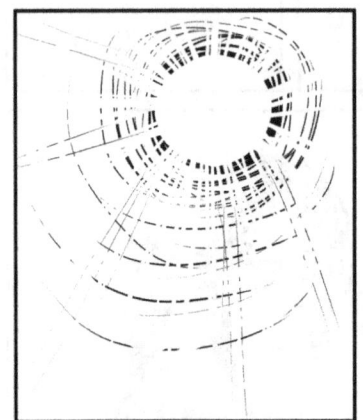

THAT, AND FIVE MINUTES OF SUNSHINE.

THIS WAS ONE OF HER BEST DAYS.

WAKING UP

NEW REALITY

ONE DAY, CONNEE FOUND HERSELF LOOKING DOWN ON HER OWN PALE, LIFELESS BODY. THERE WAS A SENSE OF NEW REALITY AND COMPASSION.

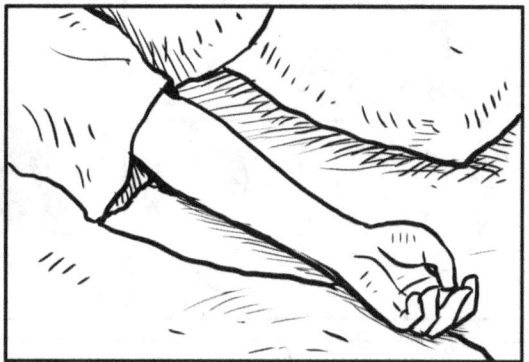

SHE SAW THE BODY'S DEBILITATION AND FRAGILITY AND FELT GREAT COMPASSION FOR IT. THERE WAS NO ONE TO BLAME FOR ITS SICKNESS.

SHE JUST HAD TO FOCUS ON MAKING HER BODY WELL.

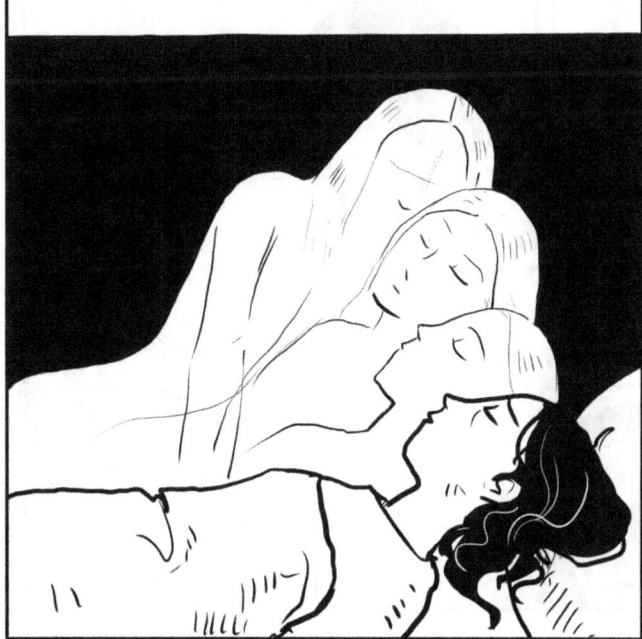

I AM SO SORRY. I DIDN'T KNOW THAT YOU DIDN'T KNOW.

I WILL TEACH YOU. FROM NOW ON, YOU WILL KNOW WHAT I WILL BE DOING AND WHAT YOU WILL BE PART OF.

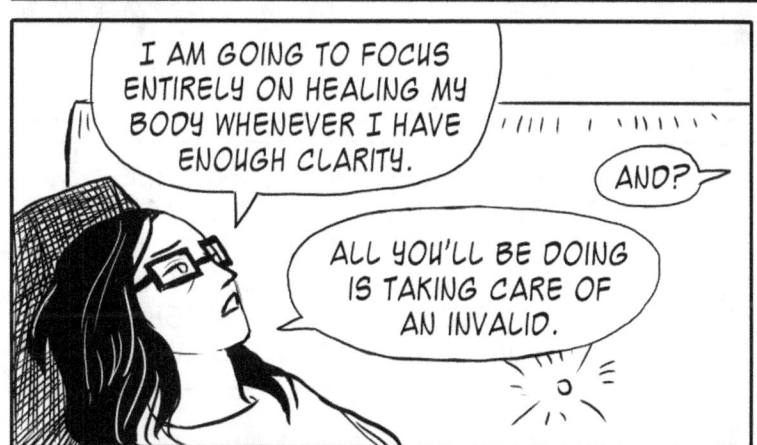

TO LEARN PROPER MEDITATION TECHNIQUES, CONNEE MET WITH MANY TEACHERS.

MANY WERE RELUCTANT TO TAKE IN SUCH A SICK PERSON LIKE HER. THEY PREFERRED A HEALTHIER MEMBER FOR THEIR CLASSES.

EVENTUALLY, CONNEE FOUND TWO MEDITATION TEACHERS WHO WERE WILLING TO TEACH SOMEONE IN HER CONDITION.

THEY RECOGNIZED THE BODY'S SICKNESS AS A MANIFESTATION OF THE SOUL.

ONE WAS FROM A MEDITATION CENTER IN THE CITY.

THE OTHER WAS A PRIVATE TEACHER.

THE PRIVATE MEDITATION TEACHER PROVIDED AS MUCH TRAINING AS CONNEE NEEDED FOR HER BODY TO UNDERSTAND.

LOST

ONE DAY CONNEE FOUND HERSELF IN THE WOMEN'S CLOTHING SECTION, WITH HEAVY FOG SHROUDING HER MIND. SHE DIDN'T KNOW WHERE SHE WAS OR WHY.

CONNEE RECOGNIZED THAT SHE HAD KEYS IN HER HAND, BUT HAD NO CLUE AS TO WHAT SHE WAS SUPPOSED TO DO WITH THEM.
WHEN SHE SAW PEOPLE EXIT THROUGH SLIDING DOORS, CONNEE WONDERED WHERE THEY WERE GOING. SHE FOLLOWED THEM OUTSIDE AND FOUND HERSELF JUST AS LOST AS BEFORE.

"WHY AM I HERE, AND WHAT AM I SUPPOSED TO DO?"

CONNEE LOOKED AROUND FOR A CLUE. SHE SPOTTED A CAR THAT LOOKED FAMILIAR.

"THE KEY FITS."

"CLUES..."

"IS THIS ME?"

CONNEE COULD NOT BELIEVE HOW HELPLESS SHE HAD BECOME.

SEARING PAIN SOMETIMES SHOT THROUGH HER ENTIRE BODY.

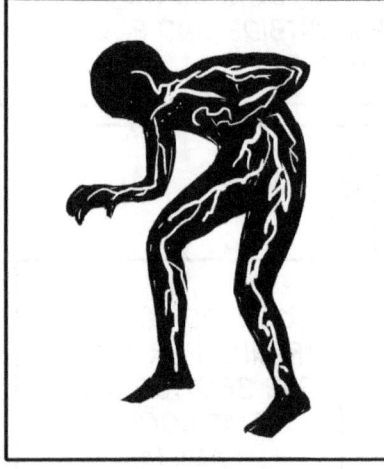

SHE LOST FIVE INCHES IN HEIGHT.

HER MIND CAME AND WENT.

CONNEE TOLD HERSELF THAT SHE'D FIND A WAY TO RECOVER HER ORIGINAL BODY.

OVER THE NEXT TWO YEARS, CONNEE'S CONDITION IMPROVED. THE SEVERITY OF HER SYMPTOMS DECREASED AND SHE HAD MORE WAKING MOMENTS. HER MEMORY SYSTEM WAS STILL BROKEN, BUT WHAT LITTLE SHE WAS ABLE TO REMEMBER SHE MADE SURE TO BE VITAL INFORMATION.

DURING CONNEE'S ILLNESS, FAMILY MEMBERS AND FRIENDS WERE ASKED TO STAY AWAY. THE WORK OF MAINTAINING RELATIONSHIPS WAS TOO MUCH FOR HER BODY. A FEW OF THEM CAME ANYWAY, NOT KNOWING THAT IT TOOK HER A WEEK TO PHYSICALLY RECOVER FROM EACH VISIT. AND SHE REFUSED HELP FROM ALL OF THEM BECAUSE WHAT THEY OFFERED COULDN'T MAKE HER WELL, AND SHE DIDN'T WANT TO BECOME DEPENDENT AND REMAIN A CRIPPLE FOREVER.

THE CELESTIAL VISIT

ONE DAY, JACK AND CONNEE WENT OUT FOR A DRIVE AND FOUND A PEACEFUL SPOT WHERE CONNEE COULD REST AND SOAK UP THE WARM SUN. SHE SLEPT UNINTERRUPTED FOR SIX HOURS.

"OH, YOU'RE UP. YOU LOOK RESTED."

THE LOGICAL MIND 1

SLOWLY, CONNEE FOUND ENOUGH STRENGTH TO FOLLOW HER LOGICAL MIND. SHE MET WITH MORE DOCTORS. THOUGH EVERYONE HAD AN OPINION, NONE OF IT WAS HELPFUL. WHAT SHE WAS FEELING AND EXPERIENCING WAS ILLOGICAL.

ONE OF HER DOCTORS SUGGESTED THAT THE CAUSE OF HER ILLNESS MIGHT BE MORE PSYCHOLOGICAL. THE DOCTOR RECOMMENDED THAT CONNEE SEEK OUT A PSYCHIATRIST.

I THINK YOU ARE DEPRESSED AND IT'S THE ROOT OF YOUR SYMPTOMS. LET'S TRY PROZAC.

I'M NOT DEPRESSED. I WOULD KNOW IF I WAS.

I AM JUST SICK.

LET'S TRY IT FOR TWO WEEKS.

....
ONE WEEK.

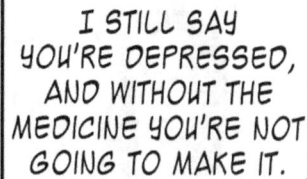

DESPITE THE STEADY WEIGHT GAIN, THE DOCTOR TOLD CONNEE TO CONTINUE TAKING THE PILLS. HE DIDN'T THINK THE PILLS WERE CAUSING HER TO GAIN WEIGHT.

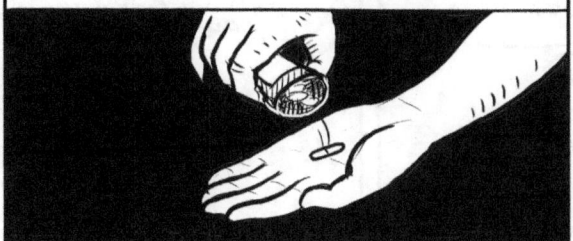

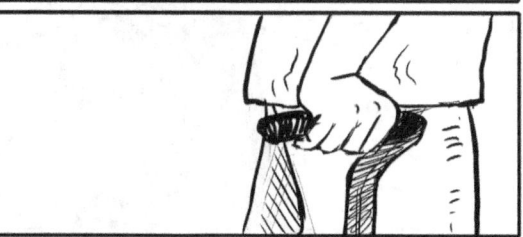

UPON THE DOCTOR'S INSISTENCE, HOPING THAT HE WAS RIGHT, SHE CONTINUED TO TAKE THE SODIUM PILLS.

I NEED TO CANCEL OUR NEXT APPOINTMENT. THANK YOU FOR TRYING, BUT I DON'T THINK YOU KNOW MY BODY LIKE I DO.

CONNEE GAINED A TOTAL OF FORTY-FIVE POUNDS.

THIS IS VERY REGRETTABLE. I HAD HOPED TO HELP YOU.

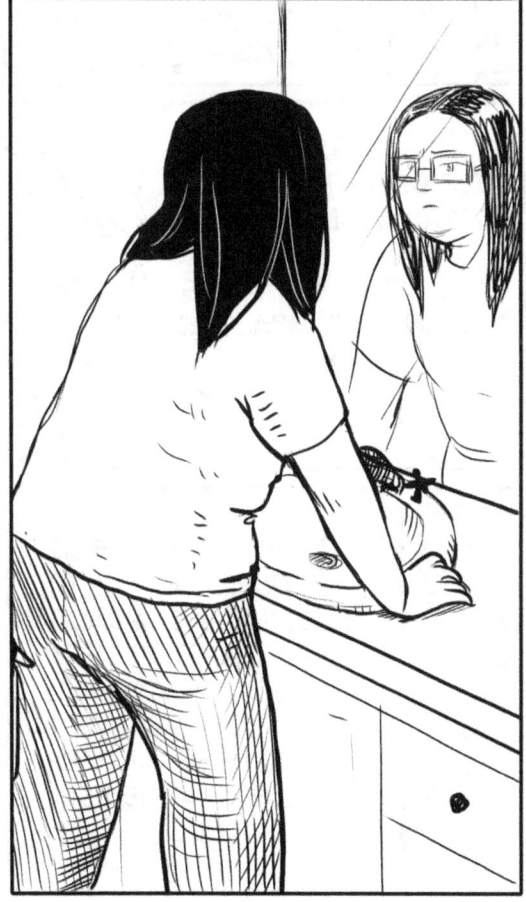

I KNOW YOU MEANT WELL, BUT GAINING AN EXTRA FORTY-FIVE POUNDS ISN'T SOMETHING I NEED RIGHT NOW.

As the recipient of Jack's unfailing kindness, Connee felt compelled to confront him again.

Jack drove Connee to all the places she needed to go. He never once complained.

THE WISE DOCTOR

CONNEE FOUND A NEUROLOGIST WHO SPECIALIZED IN ALLERGIES. HE WAS SOMEONE WHO HAD INFINITE COMPASSION FOR OTHERS' SUFFERING. AFTER MANY VISITS, THE DOCTOR QUIETLY SHARED HIS THOUGHTS. HE COULDN'T PINPOINT ANY SPECIFIC DISEASES, AND IT WAS SUCH A MULTITUDE OF SYMPTOMS FROM SO MANY MAJOR ILLNESSES THAT HE CONSIDERED IT A MIRACLE THAT SHE WAS STILL ALIVE. THE DOCTOR SPOKE GENTLY.

"DOCTORS ARE NOT GODS. WE STUDY, UNDERSTAND, AND TREAT WHAT'S ALREADY BEEN ESTABLISHED AND FOLLOW WHAT WORKS. YOURS IS AN UNKNOWN TERRITORY RIGHT NOW, BUT WE ARE WORKING HARD TO FIND THE CURE."

WHAT HE SAID SOMEHOW SOOTHED CONNEE.

"RESEARCHERS ARE DISCOVERING NEW TREATMENTS ALL THE TIME. PATIENTS WHO SHARE SOME OF YOUR SYMPTOMS HAVE BENEFITTED GREATLY FROM A TREATMENT THAT JUST CAME OUT."

"LIKE, HOW DID THEY BENEFIT?"

"THE PATIENTS GAINED MORE CLARITY. THEY HAD LESS BLURRED VISION AND FEWER BOUTS OF LONG SLEEP."

"WHAT ABOUT THE PAINS?"

"THERE'S NOTHING ELSE AT THIS TIME, BUT NEW TREATMENTS ARE COMING OUT CONSTANTLY."

"THANK YOU. I TRUST YOU, SO I WILL TRY IT."

THE DOCTOR MADE SURE CONNEE KNEW THAT THIS WAS NOT A CURE.

THE INJECTIONS WERE DONE WEEKLY AT A CLINIC NEAR HER HOME. EVERYTIME SHE WENT IN, THE STAFF HAD A DIFFICULT TIME FINDING A VEIN FOR THE INJECTIONS. SOMETIMES, THEY HAD TO USE VEINS ON HER FINGERS AND TOES. THIS MADE IT PAINFUL FOR CONNEE, BUT SHE APPRECIATED THEIR HELP NEVERTHELESS.

AFTER SEVERAL MONTHS INTO THE TREATMENT, THEY COULDN'T FIND ANY MORE VEINS.

THE DOCTOR CHANGED THE TREATMENT TO SELF-ADMINISTERED INJECTIONS TO THE REAR.

CONNEE STARTED TO FEEL BETTER. THE PAIN WAS STILL THERE, BUT SHE NO LONGER HAD BLURRED VISION AND COULD FOCUS LONGER. SIMPLY HAVING MORE CLARITY FELT CLOSE TO A CURE FOR HER. SHE WAS GOING FROM A NONFUNCTIONAL BEING TO A SOMEWHAT FUNCTIONAL BEING. COMPARED TO THREE YEARS AGO, CONNEE'S CONDITION HAD CHANGED GREATLY.

NOW, SHE COULD TAKE SMALL TRIPS WITH JACK'S HELP, EVEN IF SHE STILL SLEPT MOST OF THE TIME.

THE LECTURE

OVER THE COURSE OF HER ILLNESS, CONNEE RECOGNIZED HER BODY'S DEBILITATION AS A CALL TO CHANGE HER LIFE'S TRAJECTORY. IT WAS POINTING HER TOWARDS "HOME", WHEREVER THAT WAS. AND SHE WOULD SOLELY RELY ON THE GUIDANCE OF HER INNER VOICE TO REACH HER DESTINATION. THAT GUIDANCE HAD CONNEE ATTEND A TALK IN SEATTLE BY A VISITING ZEN MASTER.

BEGINNING TO SLIP IN AND OUT OF CONSCIOUSNESS, CONNEE HAD TO ASK HER QUESTION.

BRUSHING OFF THE DISAPPOINTING ENCOUNTER WITH THE ZEN MASTER, CONNEE DECIDED SHE NEEDED TO GO ABROAD TO FIND HER ANSWERS.

THE CROWS

A FEW WEEKS LATER, SHE MET WITH ONE OF HER MEDITATION TEACHERS.

SHE TOLD HIM THAT SHE WAS PLANNING TO BE OUT OF THE COUNTRY FOR A WHILE.

"WITH THAT BODY?"

"YES. I HAVE TO."

"I WANTED TO THANK YOU FOR ALL YOUR TEACHINGS. YOU HAVE HELPED ME A GREAT DEAL - MORE THAN I HAD HOPED FOR."

"BEFORE YOU GO, YOU NEED TO MEET SOMEONE. I DON'T KNOW HIM PERSONALLY, BUT HE IS THE VISITING ZEN MASTER WHO DID A TALK RECENTLY."

"YES, I WENT TO ONE OF HIS LECTURES AND ASKED HIM A QUESTION. HE DIDN'T EVEN ANSWER. I NEED TO LEARN MORE BEFORE I CONSIDER GOING BACK TO HIM."

"READY OR NOT, YOU NEED TO MEET WITH HIM. ALL MY SENSES ARE TELLING ME THIS."

"I JUST DID."

"AT LEAST GIVE HIM A CALL."

"NO."

A FEW DAYS LATER, THE MEDITATION TEACHER CALLED AGAIN TO SEE IF CONNEE WOULD RECONSIDER AND SPEAK WITH THE ZEN MASTER.

RIGHT AFTER THE PHONE CALL SHE SLIPPED INTO A CYCLE OF BAD DAYS AND FORGOT TO CALL THE ZEN MASTER.

ONCE SHE RECOVERED, CONNEE MADE AN APPOINTMENT TO MEET WITH THE MEDITATION TEACHER.

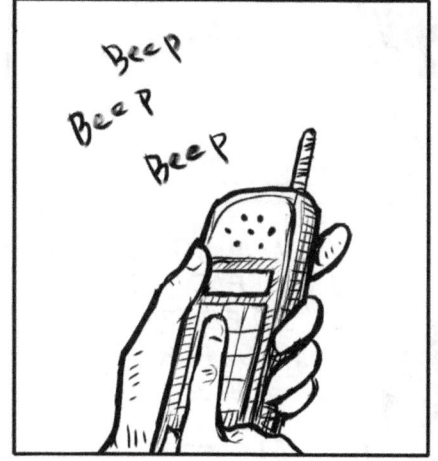

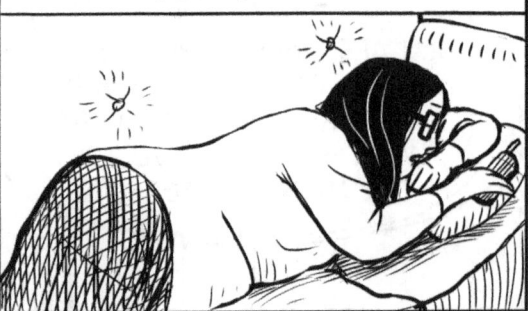

After a few weeks of telephone conversations with the Zen Master, Connee agreed to the trip. Jack made the travel arrangements.

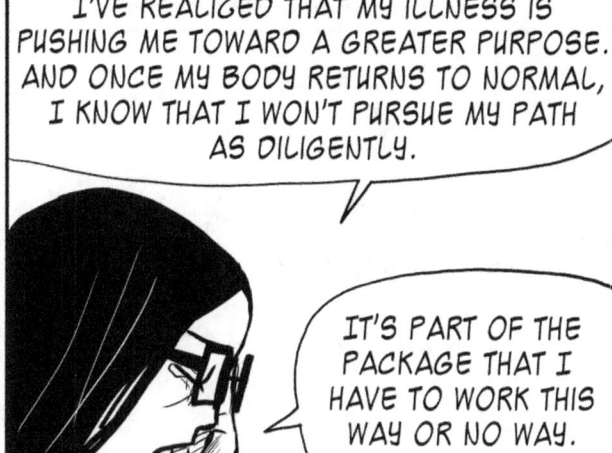

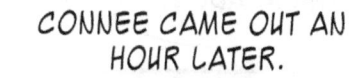

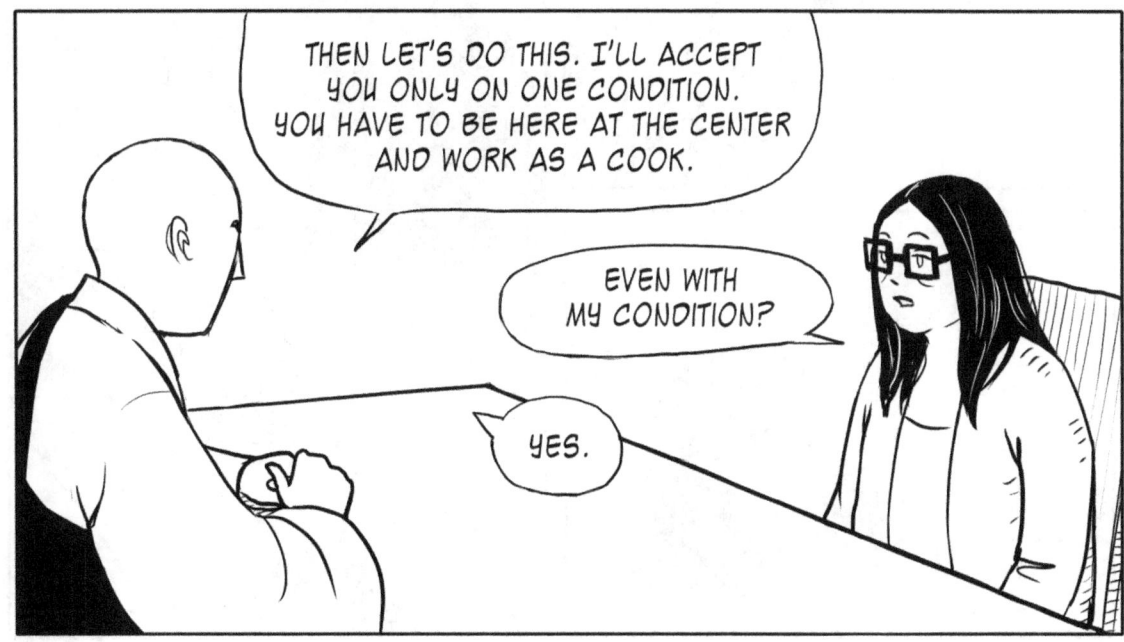

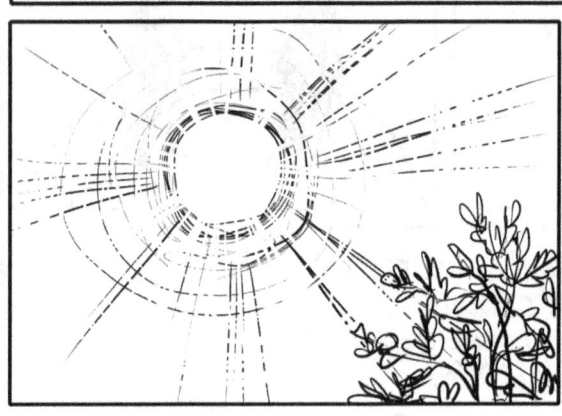

I WILL BE ENTERING A MONASTERY TO PURSUE MY LEARNING. WHAT DO YOU THINK?

IS THAT WHAT YOU WANT?

YES, I DO.

I'VE ALWAYS KNOWN THAT THIS WAS WHERE I WAS HEADED, BUT I DIDN'T WANT TO ACCEPT IT.

BUT AFTER SPEAKING WITH THE MASTER, I'VE GAINED MORE CLARITY. IT WAS INTERESTING THAT MY LIFE SEEMS TO MIRROR HIS IN MANY WAYS.

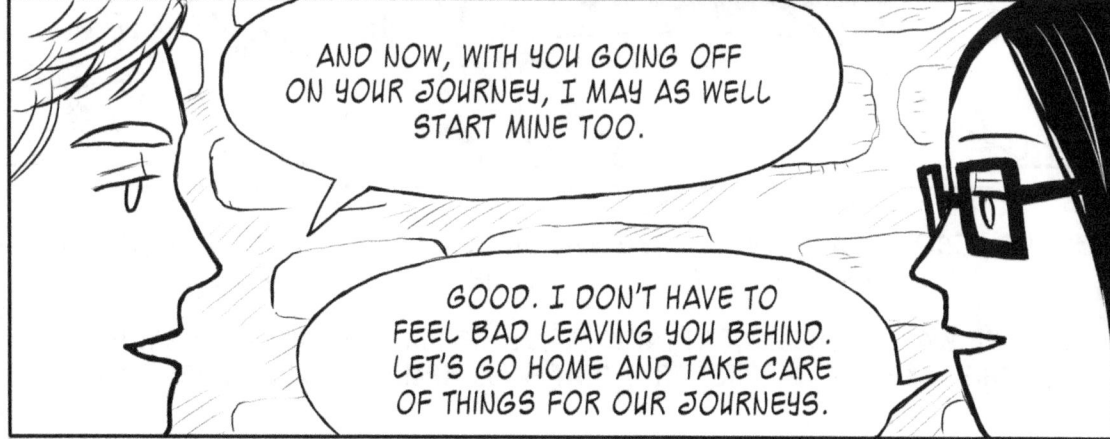

AND NOW, WITH YOU GOING OFF ON YOUR JOURNEY, I MAY AS WELL START MINE TOO.

GOOD. I DON'T HAVE TO FEEL BAD LEAVING YOU BEHIND. LET'S GO HOME AND TAKE CARE OF THINGS FOR OUR JOURNEYS.

SELLING OFF ALL

JACK SOON LEFT FOR A RETREAT. BUT BEFORE DEPARTING, JACK REQUESTED THAT CONNEE COME BACK TO SAVE HIM IF SHE WAS TO AWAKEN TO HER TRUE NATURE BEFORE HE DID. CONNEE PROMISED JACK THAT SHE'D RETURN FOR HIM.

CONNEE STAYED AT THE ZEN CENTER WHILE HER HOUSE AND THE TWENTY-ACRE PROPERTY IN LAKE CHELAN WERE PUT UP FOR SALE. BY THE TIME THE REAL ESTATE AGENT CALLED TO TELL HER THAT THE HOUSE HAD SOLD, CONNEE'S PHYSICAL CONDITION WAS GETTING PROGRESSIVELY BETTER.

CONNEE CAME BACK UP TO SEATTLE TO TAKE CARE OF HER BELONGINGS.

WITH THE HELP OF HER FRIEND SUSAN, CONNEE ORGANIZED THE SALE OF ALL HER POSSESSIONS.

APART FROM A FEW APPLIANCES TO BE USED AT THE SAN FRANCISCO CENTER, CONNEE PUT UP FOR SALE EVERYTHING SHE OWNED: INCLUDING HER CAR, FURNITURES, CLOTHING, JEWELRY, AND FIFTY PAIRS OF SHOES. SHE DIDN'T NEED ANY OF THESE THINGS WHERE SHE WAS GOING.

BY THE SECOND DAY, MOST OF THE MAJOR ITEMS WERE SOLD, AND WHAT WAS LEFT OVER WAS DROPPED OFF AT THE NEAREST THRIFT STORE.

CONNEE WAS FINISHED WITH THAT CHAPTER OF HER LIFE, WITH THE EXCEPTION OF THE LAKE CHELAN PROPERTY THAT STILL REMAINED UNDER HER NAME.

AS A CHILD RECOUNTS A STORY TO A PARENT, CONNEE DESCRIBED HER JOURNEY TO SAN FRANCISCO.

I WAS VERY HAPPY AND CONTENT TO LEAVE SEATTLE. EVERYTHING WAS GOING FINE UNTIL I BRIEFLY BLACKED OUT NEAR THE WASHINGTON STATE BORDER.

WHEN I CAME TO, THE TRUCK HAD STOPPED ON A HILL, AWAY FROM I-5. THE TRUCK WAS PARKED WITH THE ENGINE STILL RUNNING AND THE HOOD OPEN. SCARED, I DROVE DOWN THE UNEVEN HILL.

WHEN I GOT TO THE SHOULDER OF I-5, THE ENGINE DIED. THE HOOD WAS DENTED AND WOULDN'T CLOSE, AND THERE WERE MORE DENTS NEAR THE FUEL TANK. THANKFULLY, IT WASN'T LEAKING.

I KNEW NOTHING ABOUT TRUCKS. WITH THE EMERGENCY LIGHTS ON, I WAITED FOR HELP BUT NONE CAME. SO, I TRIED STARTING THE ENGINE AGAIN.

PART II

TO LEARNING AND RECOVERY

NEW LIFE

CONNEE WAS EXCITED TO LEARN UNDER THE ZEN MASTER. SHE HELPED WITH DAILY COOKING FOR ABOUT 10 - 15 PEOPLE TWICE A DAY. DESPITE HER SICK BODY, SHE GAVE HER BEST.

SEVERAL MONTHS LATER, THE ZEN MASTER CALLED CONNEE TO HIS ROOM. THERE HE TOLD HER TO GET HER NAME ON THE CENTER'S BANK ACCOUNT AS A SIGNED USER AND GAVE HER THE KEYS TO THE CENTER'S CAR.

CONNEE REFUSED.

"I'VE LET GO OF ALL MY WORLDLY RESPONSIBILITIES. I DON'T WANT THEM BACK AGAIN."

"IT'S VERY INCONVENIENT FOR OTHERS IF YOU CAN'T GO OUT AND SHOP ON YOUR OWN."

"I AM NOT HEALTHY ENOUGH TO BE TRUSTED WITH THAT."

THE ZEN MASTER GAVE CONNEE A COUPLE DAYS TO THINK IT OVER.

SHE HAD TWO OPTIONS. SHE EITHER STAYED AT THE CENTER AND ACCEPTED ALL RULES AND CONDITIONS, OR, SHE SIMPLY LEFT THE CENTER.

FOR CONNEE, IT WASN'T MUCH OF A CHOICE.

CONNEE UNHAPPILY TOOK THE CAR KEYS AND PUT HER NAME DOWN ON THE ZEN CENTER'S BANK ACCOUNT. SHE BEGAN TO BROOD.

THE UNHOLY ZEN MASTER

CONNEE WAS NOT AWARE HOW HER EMOTIONS WERE COLORING HER PERCEPTION AND ATTITUDE UNTIL ABOUT A MONTH LATER. SHE NO LONGER SAW THE ZEN MASTER AS HOLY, AND WHENEVER HE TRIED TO POINT OUT HER EMOTIONAL STATE, SHE DISMISSED HIS HELP AND ASSUMED HE WAS TRYING TO JUSTIFY HIS ACTIONS.

HER FEELINGS AND THOUGHTS FROM HER LOGICAL MIND SEEMED JUSTIFIED, YET SOMETHING ABOUT IT BOTHERED HER.

ONE DAY, AT A ZEN SITTING, SHE REALIZED THAT FOR A MOMENT, SHE DIDN'T HAVE EMOTION AND LOGIC PRESENT.

ALL SHE FELT WAS PEACE.

THE HERB PANTRY

One day, the Zen Master put Connee in charge of the herb pantry and its duties.

He identified each herb, explaining how it worked and what body type should be taking them.

"The most important thing is to care for the person. One neglect could cause more suffering and even death. So, it's crucial to pay attention to the mind that prepares the dosages."

"My health isn't stable. I cannot take responsibility for someone else's life."

"Become familiar with the pantry, and also do some cleaning. Remember, only you and two other people are allowed here."

Barely able to keep up with all her duties, she was becoming exhausted.

Nevertheless, she gave it her best.

As she worked, thoughts ran through her head.

"This isn't learning. This is abuse. This isn't what I came here to do. Does he know that the herb smell makes me sick?"

After her duties in the herb pantry, Connee went to the Zen Master's office, still weak from the smell of the herbs.

"So, do you see a solution?"

Connee noticed that the Zen Master's wholesome energy permeated into her sick body, melting away her exhaustion and resentment.

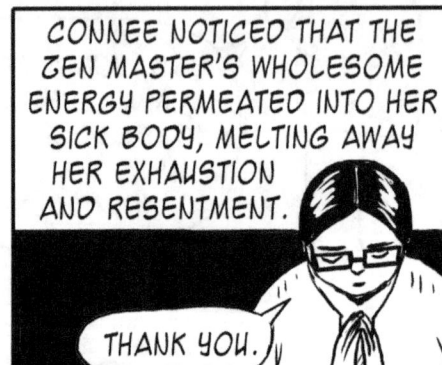

"Thank you."

"I am getting stronger everyday."

"Without a healthy body, you cannot reach where you want to go."

"I understand now. I will keep a meditative mind while I prepare the herbs."

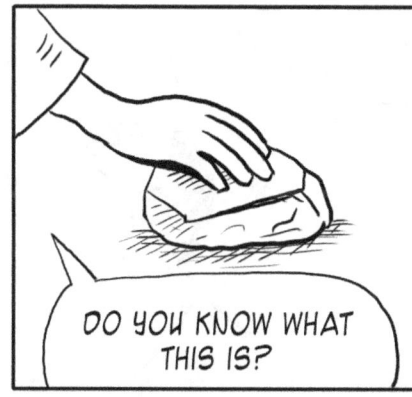

FIVE ORGANS AND THEIR FUNCTION

ENTRUST EVERYTHING TO YOUR TRUE NATURE. HOWEVER, AN UNBALANCED BODY CAN PREVENT YOU FROM DOING EXACTLY THAT.

IT'S YOUR DUTY TO KNOW HOW YOUR BODY OPERATES. SOMETIMES, IT'S A MATTER OF DOING MINOR THINGS TO PREVENT MAJOR PROBLEMS. SOMETIMES, IT'S A MAJOR ISSUE. EITHER WAY, YOU NEED TO LEARN TO KNOW YOUR BODY. IT IS YOUR VESSEL AND AFFECTS YOUR SPIRITUAL JOURNEY AS WELL. ONCE THE BODY LOSES HARMONY, ILLNESS SETS IN. THE BODY IS FOLLOWING PHYSICAL LAWS.

YOU ARE LIVING WITH FIVE THIEVES.
NAME THEM.

I'M LIVING WITH THIEVES?

YES, LET'S GO THROUGH EACH.

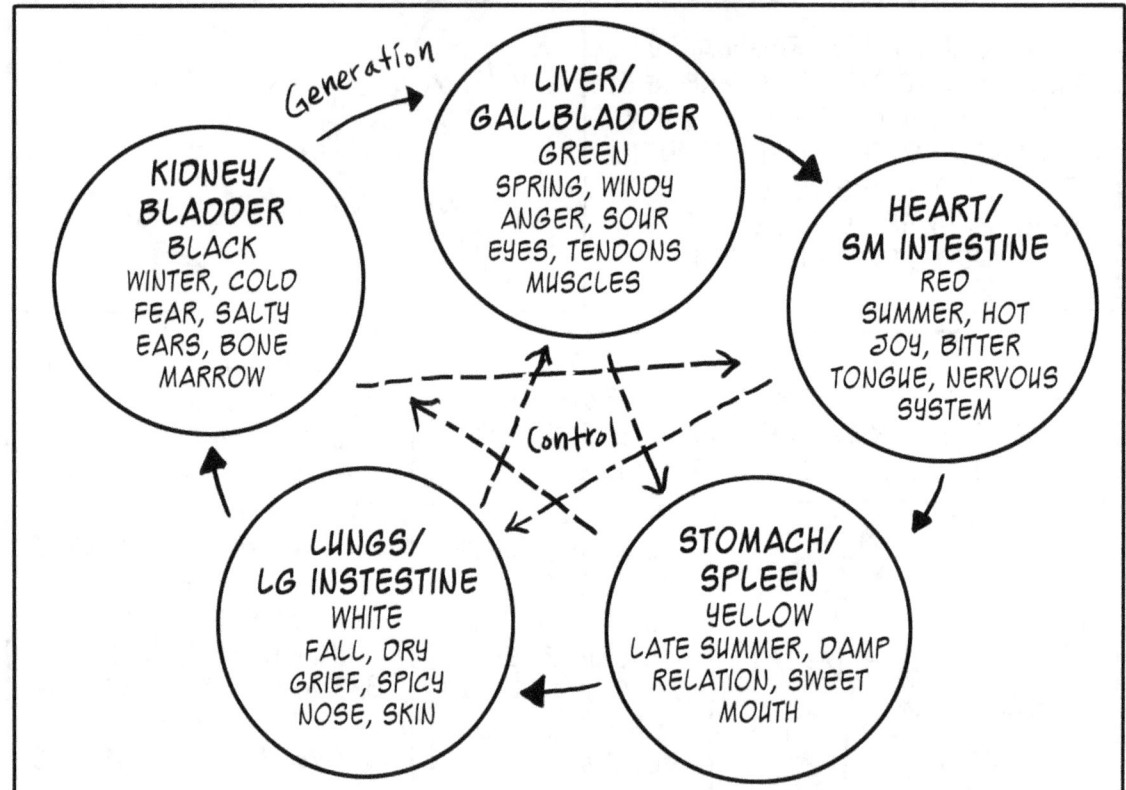

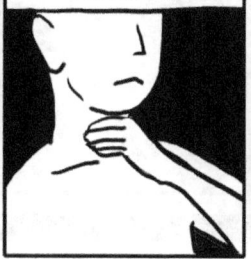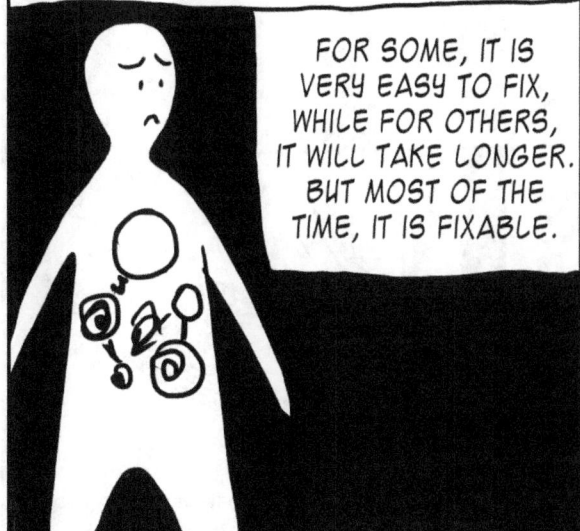

THE WISE COUNTRY DOCTOR

"PEOPLE DON'T PAY ATTENTION BECAUSE THEY ARE YOUNG AND IGNORANT. I, TOO, WAS YOUNG AND IGNORANT. I WAS DETERMINED TO ACHIEVE SPIRITUAL ENLIGHTENMENT SO I DID RIGOROUS ZEN RETREATS UNTIL HEALTH PROBLEMS FINALLY STOPPED ME."

"ALL CONCEPTS FROM MY HEAD DIDN'T WORK, NOR DID MODERN MEDICINE. ONLY AN OLD HERBALIST OUT IN THE MIDDLE OF NOWHERE..."

"DO YOU WANT TO HEAR WHY I BECAME AN HERBALIST?"

"YES!"

I WAS 18 AND ENTERED THE MONASTERY THINKING THAT I WOULD LEARN UNDER THE GREAT ZEN MASTERS AND BECOME AN ENLIGHTENED BEING. THAT WAS MY GOAL.

I ATTENDED ALL THE ZEN RETREATS DILIGENTLY AND WHOLEHEARTEDLY. THEN MY BODY STARTED BREAKING DOWN AND INTERFERING WITH MY ZEN STUDY.

I HAD NOTICED THAT SOME PRACTIONERS ALSO QUIT DUE TO THEIR HEALTH. BUT I WASN'T GOING TO BE LIKE THAT! I THOUGHT THEY WERE WEAK, UNABLE TO FINISH WHAT THEY STARTED. THERE WERE PRACTITIONERS WHO HAD NO PROBLEM ENDURING THE LONG HOURS OF MEDITATION THAT WENT THROUGH THE NIGHT FOR DAYS ON END.

MY JOINTS WERE BREAKING DOWN FROM SITTING SO LONG. THE PAIN INTERFERED WITH MY FOCUS. ALL MY ENERGIES SEEMED TO RISE INSTEAD OF CALMING DOWN FOR MEDITATION. I ASKED THE ZEN MASTERS ABOUT IT, BUT TO NO AVAIL.

UNFORTUNATELY, MY PROBLEM WAS SEEN AS A SIGN OF WEAKNESS TO THEM, SOMETHING I MYSELF HAD THOUGHT WHEN I SAW IT IN OTHERS.
BUT I KNEW I WASN'T WEAK. I JUST HAD A PROBLEM.

DESPITE MY PROBLEM, I CONTINUED TO ENTER ZEN RETREATS 100 DAYS AT A TIME, TWICE A YEAR. EVENTUALLY, EVEN MY BACK GAVE OUT, MAKING IT IMPOSSIBLE FOR ME TO CONTINUE.

THE PATRONS OF THE MONASTERY PROVIDED ME WITH ALL THE BEST THINGS THAT MONEY COULD BUY TO HELP ME GET BETTER. THAT ACTUALLY MADE IT WORSE. I FINALLY TALKED WITH MY ZEN MASTER AND INFORMED HIM THAT I NEEDED TIME OFF TO FIND TREATMENT AND THEN RETURN TO THE MONASTERY. I RECEIVED HIS PERMISSION.

I WENT TO MANY SPECIALISTS AND SEEMED TO IMPROVE SOMEWHAT, BUT THAT WAS IT.

AFTER SIX MONTHS I WENT BACK TO THE MONASTERY AND ENTERED A 100 DAY RETREAT. THE PAIN WAS SO UNBEARABLE THAT I BARELY FINISHED IT.
I PRAYED AND PRAYED FOR SOMEONE TO HELP ME WITH MY PAIN. I WAS A WOUNDED WARRIOR, AND I DIDN'T LIKE THAT AT ALL.

ONE DAY, I WAS WALKING DOWN A COUNTRY ROAD WITHOUT ANY HOPE OF GETTING BETTER. I PASSED THROUGH A SMALL VILLAGE AND NEAR THE ROAD I SAW AN OLD HOUSE WITH A SIGN THAT READ "HERBAL DOCTOR".

I NOTICED THAT HIS EYES WERE PARTICULARLY ALIVE. I BEGAN SHARING MY HEALTH PROBLEMS. HE LISTENED CAREFULLY AND TOLD ME THAT WE EACH HAVE UNIQUE SIGNATURES AS INDIVIDUALS. ONE COULDN'T TREAT A PERSON WITHOUT KNOWING THAT UNIQUE SIGNATURE. SOMETIMES, ONE CAN GET LUCKY BY SIMPLY GUESSING OR USING TRIAL AND ERROR TO FIND A CURE TO THE ILLNESS.

THE HERBALIST TOLD ME THAT HE COULD TREAT ME AND INVITED ME TO STAY WITH HIM. SINCE THERE WAS NO EXTRA ROOM, I WOULD HAVE TO STAY IN THE TINY HERB ROOM WHERE I COULD BARELY LAY DOWN.

I ASKED HIM HOW HE WAS GOING TO TREAT ME. HE SAID THAT HE COULD SEE THROUGH MY BODY. HE DIDN'T NEED ANY BOOK OR MEDICAL EQUIPMENT.

I WAS INTRIGUED. I HAD NOTHING TO LOSE, SO I ACCEPTED HIS OFFER.

MY BODY RESPONDED WITHIN DAYS. ON THE THIRD DAY, HE STUCK LONG ACUPUNCTURE NEEDLES INTO MY BODY. I DIDN'T FEEL ANY PAIN AFTER THAT. IT WAS UNBELIEVABLE. I STAYED WITH HIM UNTIL THE NEXT ZEN RETREAT TIME, LEARNING SO MUCH UNDER HIS CARE.

I FINISHED THE RETREAT WITHOUT PROBLEM. AFTERWARDS, I WENT BACK TO THE OLD HERBALIST. HE WAS GLAD TO SEE ME. I WAS UNDER HIS CARE UNTIL THE NEXT RETREAT.

ACCORDING TO HIM, WE ALL HAVE DIFFERENT BODY TYPES. HIS TREATMENT IS BASED ON THE BODY TYPES WHILE HIS ACUPUNCTURE IS BASED ON THE CYCLE OF THE UNIVERSE. IT WAS SOMETHING I KNEW NOTHING ABOUT.

ONE DAY, I ASKED HIM HOW I SHOULD ADDRESS HIM. HE SAID "OLD MAN" WAS FINE. HE SAID HE WAS IN HIS NINETIES. I COULDN'T BELIEVE IT. I WAS IN MY EARLY TWENTIES AND YET HE WAS HEALTHIER THAN I WAS. I ASKED HIM HOW HE HAD KEPT HIMSELF SO YOUNG. HE TOLD ME THAT HE HAD PRACTICED TAOIST SUN DOH YOGA MEDITATION FOR A LONG TIME. HE SUGGESTED THAT I LEARN IT WHEN THE OPPORTUNITY AROSE.

HE SAID TAOIST SUN DOH YOGA WAS AN ANCIENT PRACTICE THAT HAS EXISTED ONLY THROUGH WORD OF MOUTH. I HAD NEVER HEARD OF THIS. FORTUNATELY, WHEN I LATER SEARCHED FOR IT, I FOUND OUT THAT SOMEONE HAD ALREADY BROUGHT IT OUT TO THE PUBLIC. THAT'S ANOTHER TALE.

ANYWAY, THIS MAN IN HIS NINETIES WAS THE ONE WHO TAUGHT ME WHAT I KNOW NOW AND HAS ALLOWED ME TO TREAT YOUR ILLNESS.

HOWEVER, SIMPLY RECEIVING WON'T BE ENOUGH. YOU WILL NEED TO LEARN THIS FOR YOURSELF AND YOUR INDEPENDENCE. AND I KNOW HOW MUCH YOU LOVE YOUR INDEPENDENCE.

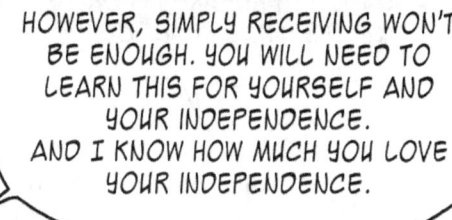

THANK YOU. BUT LEARNING THOSE THINGS ISN'T WHAT I NEED TO BE DOING AT THIS TIME.

YOU NEED TO LEARN TO TAKE CARE OF YOUR BODY. IT'S YOUR JOB TO KNOW HOW IT OPERATES SO YOU KNOW WHAT TO DO WHEN THINGS GO WRONG. OF COURSE YOU CAN TAKE MODERN DRUGS TO EASE THE SYMPTOMS, BUT DOCTORS CAN ONLY DO CERTAIN THINGS. THE JOB OF MAINTAINING THE BODY IS YOURS.

ANYWAY, I FOLLOWED HIS RECOMMENDED DIET AND AVOIDED ALL FOODS THAT WERE NOT BENEFICIAL TO MY BODY TYPE. NO MATTER HOW TEMPTING CERTAIN FOODS WERE.

AS A ZEN PRACTITIONER, I WAS SUPPOSED TO ACCEPT WHAT WAS OFFERED TO ME. STILL, I POLITELY REFUSED THE FOODS OFFERED TO ME BY TEMPLE PATRONS, CITING HEALTH REASONS. MY EXCUSES SOMETIMES WORKED, AND SOMETIMES IT JUST SEEMED RUDE AND UN-PRACTITIONER-LIKE.

AT THE RETREATS, ONLY CERTAIN TYPES OF FOODS WERE AVAILABLE SO I CHOSE CAREFULLY ACCORDING TO MY BODY TYPE. I GOT HUNGRY SOMETIMES, BUT I WASN'T SICK. AND SURE ENOUGH, WHEN I DIDN'T PAY ATTENTION AND FORGOT, I WOULD BE SICK FROM EATING THE WRONG FOODS. THIS NOTICEABLY AFFECTED MY MEDITATION PRACTICE. SO, I LEARNED TO AVOID ALL FOODS THAT BROKE HARMONY IN ME. I WAS DETERMINED TO BECOME AN ENLIGHTENED BEING, AFTER ALL.

THE HERBALIST TAUGHT ME THAT EVEN THOUGH SO MANY ARE EAGER TO DO ZEN TRAINING, SOME WERE NOT BUILT TO ENDURE ITS HARDSHIPS. I MYSELF DIDN'T UNDERSTAND BODY AND ZEN. THE HERBALIST POINTED OUT THAT IF ONE TAKES THE CAR OUT FOR A LONG JOURNEY, ONE SHOULD AT LEAST KNOW SOMETHING ABOUT FIXING THE CAR, IN CASE ONE GETS STUCK ON AN UNKNOWN ROAD. WITH NO ONE TO HELP YOU, IT WOULD BE A WISE THING TO KNOW AND PREPARE. HE SAID SIMPLY SITTING IN MEDITATION WASN'T ZEN.

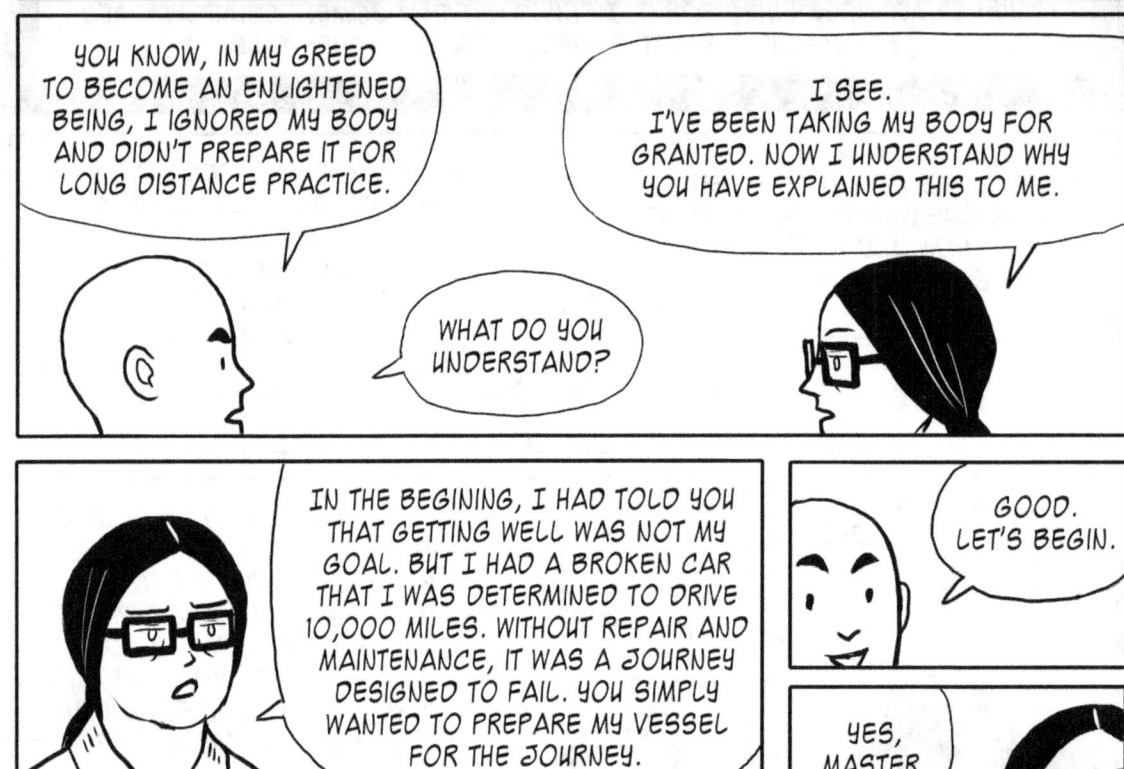

YOU KNOW, IN MY GREED TO BECOME AN ENLIGHTENED BEING, I IGNORED MY BODY AND DIDN'T PREPARE IT FOR LONG DISTANCE PRACTICE.

I SEE. I'VE BEEN TAKING MY BODY FOR GRANTED. NOW I UNDERSTAND WHY YOU HAVE EXPLAINED THIS TO ME.

WHAT DO YOU UNDERSTAND?

IN THE BEGINING, I HAD TOLD YOU THAT GETTING WELL WAS NOT MY GOAL. BUT I HAD A BROKEN CAR THAT I WAS DETERMINED TO DRIVE 10,000 MILES. WITHOUT REPAIR AND MAINTENANCE, IT WAS A JOURNEY DESIGNED TO FAIL. YOU SIMPLY WANTED TO PREPARE MY VESSEL FOR THE JOURNEY.

GOOD. LET'S BEGIN.

YES, MASTER.

REFLECT AND REPENT/SELF-KNOWING

THE ZEN MASTER TAUGHT CONNEE EVERY DAY SO THAT SHE COULD PRACTICE WHAT SHE HAD LEARNED. HE PRESCRIBED HERB FORMULAS AND TAUGHT HER DIET, ZEN, AND TAOIST SUN DOH BREATHING AND YOGA. HER ILLNESS MADE HER FORGET A LOT OF THINGS AND MADE EVERYTHING MORE DIFFICULT, BUT SHE FOLLOWED WHAT SHE COULD.

ONE DAY, THE ZEN MASTER BECAME FURIOUS WHILE SHE SERVED TEA.

GET OUT! YOU CAN'T STAY AT THE CENTER. THIS IS NOT ACCEPTABLE!

I AM SORRY. OBVIOUSLY, I MADE YOU MAD, BUT I DON'T UNDERSTAND WHAT I DID WRONG JUST NOW. PLEASE TELL ME.

DO NOT KNOW? DO NOT KNOW! GET OUT!

HE WAS SO LIVID THAT CONNEE HAD TO LEAVE THE ROOM.

CONNEE SAT OUTSIDE HIS OFFICE FOR HOURS.

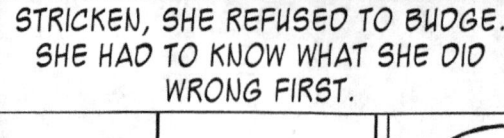

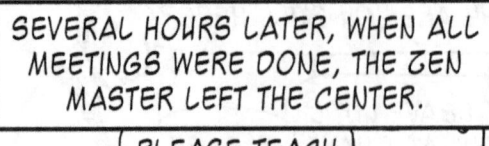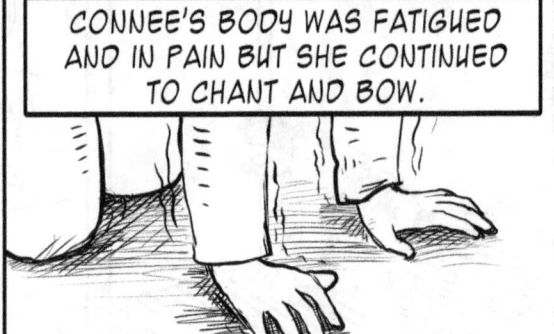

THE HEAD-SHAVING CEREMONY

  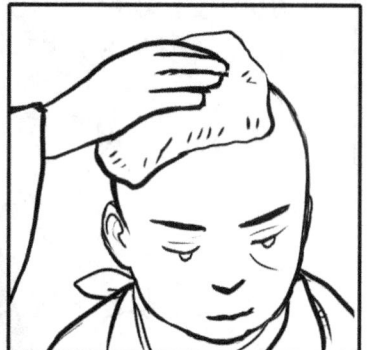

AS A SIGN OF LETTING GO OF ALL HABITS OF THE OUTSIDE WORLD, THE ZEN MASTER SHAVED CONNEE'S HEAD. THIS WOULD MARK THE BEGINNING OF A NEW BLANK PAGE IN CONNEE'S LIFE JOURNEY.

AFTER THE CEREMONY, ALL CONNEE FELT WAS FREE. ALL WORLDLY ISSUES WERE BEHIND HER, AND IT MADE HER HAPPY. WHATEVER WAS ASKED OF HER, SHE SAID YES TO BECAUSE IT SOMEHOW FELT RIGHT.

CONNEE DECIDED THAT THE SHAVED HEAD WAS HER BEST LOOK YET. THERE WAS NOTHING TO MAINTAIN AND NOTHING TO EMBELLISH.

SO CONNEE SHARED HER EXPERIENCES. HER CLAIMS FASCINATED THE ZEN MASTER AS HE HAD NEVER HEARD OF SUCH THINGS HAPPENING TO ANYONE. TO PROVE HER CLAIM, SHE LAID OUT EVIDENCE BEFORE HIS EYES AND AGAINST ALL HIS KNOWLEDGE. CONNEE TOLD HIM THAT SHE HAD NO DESIRE TO USE OR MISUSE THE CONTENTS OF HER EXPERIENCES. SHE ONLY DESIRED TO REACH HER ULTIMATE DESTINATION—HOME.

CONNEE DESCRIBED THE CONTENTS OF HER VISIONS AS HE LISTENED INTENTLY. AT ONE POINT, HE INTERRUPTED TO CLAIM THAT HE WAS ONE OF THE FIGURES FROM THE VISION. CONNEE STOPPED THE STORY AS SHE COULDN'T TELL HIM THE REST.

     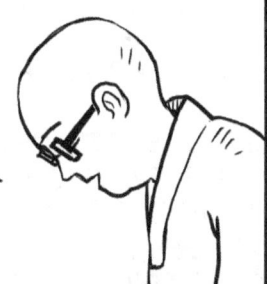

EATING OUT WITH THE ZEN MASTER

One night, the Zen Master had Connee accompany him to a restaurant. When the wait person came, he ordered his food.

Connee ordered a salad while the Zen Master ordered a hamburger with everything on it, except for onions. Connee found this odd and unfair.

Why did he get to eat the huge burger while she had to eat a salad because it was late? Eating this late would have been terrible for anyone, so why was the Zen Master eating at this hour?

This didn't make sense to Connee, but she did not share her thoughts with the Zen Master. Connee kept her growing discontent to herself, especially with the Zen Master enjoying his burger like it was an amazing feast.

ONE DAY, THEY WENT TO A RESTAURANT OWNED BY ONE OF THE ZEN MASTER'S STUDENTS. THE OWNER WAS HAPPY TO SEE HIM AND ORDERED HIS FAVORITE HAMBURGER FOR HIM. THEN THE OWNER ASKED CONNEE WHAT SHE WANTED.

THE ZEN MASTER DIDN'T EXPLAIN HIS ACTIONS AT THE RESTAURANT. HE JUST CONTINUED TO DO THE SAME THING AT ALL ODD HOURS OF THE DAY. HE WOULD CALL HER AND SAY THAT HE WAS HUNGRY AND HAVE HER ACCOMPANY HIM. CONNEE WOULD THEN LOOK FORWARD TO EATING OUT SINCE IT DIDN'T HAPPEN OFTEN AND HAD FORGOTTEN THE PREVIOUS INCIDENTS BY THEN.

ONE MORNING, CONNEE EAGERLY FOLLOWED THE ZEN MASTER OUT FOR BREAKFAST. AGAIN, HE ORDERED FOOD FOR HIMSELF BUT NONE FOR HER. SHE JUST SIPPED HER WATER AS HE SHARED MANY STORIES ABOUT PEOPLE AND THEIR ISSUES, USING THEM AS A TEACHING TOOL FOR CONNEE. MEANWHILE, ANGRY THOUGHTS RAGED IN CONNEE'S HEAD AS HER STRESS LEVELS ESCALATED.

HERE SHE WAS, CLUELESS AS TO WHAT WAS GOING ON, AND STARVED FOR BREAKFAST SHE WAS NOT ALLOWED TO EAT. WHILE HE TOLD OTHERS THAT SHE WAS ILL AND FORGETFUL, HE HIMSELF WAS SHOWING NO CONSIDERATION FOR HER AND NOT ONCE MENTIONING THE REASON BEHIND HER EMPTY PLATE. HE JUST CONTINUED TO TALK TO HER ABOUT SOME OTHER PERSON'S ISSUES AND ASK FOR HER OPINIONS!

UNABLE TO KEEP SILENT ANY LONGER, CONNEE TOLD HIM HOW SHE FELT ABOUT THE FOOD SITUATION—VERY LOGICALLY. THE ZEN MASTER RAISED HIS VOICE AND WAVED AN OUTRAGED FINGER AT HER, AS IF SHE HAD DONE SOMETHING TERRIBLE.

THE ZEN MASTER CALMED DOWN. CONNEE DIDN'T KNOW WHAT TO SAY EXCEPT TO APOLOGIZE. SOMETHING HAD GONE WRONG BUT SHE DIDN'T KNOW WHAT IT WAS. SHE HAD NO CLUE HOW TO CORRECT IT.

THE ZEN MASTER ATE HIS MEAL IN SILENCE AS CONNEE TRIED TO FIGURE OUT WHAT ALL THIS MEANT. SHE QUIETLY WATCHED HIM ENJOY HIS MEAL. THEN SHE SAW THAT ALL THIS TIME, SHE HAD REACTED NOT WITH THE PRACTITIONER'S MINDFULNESS BUT WITH LOGIC AND EMOTION.

CONNEE HAD REALIZED HER PROBLEM.

AT DAWN, THE ENERGY IS MOST CLEAR AND CRISP. IT PROVIDES TREMENDOUS LIVER ENERGY, WHICH IS LIFE/SPRING ENERGY.

NOON IS LIKE SUMMER.

AFTERNOON BEFORE DINNER IS LIKE FALL

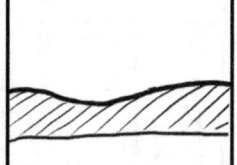
AFTER 7PM IS PRE-WINTER AND WINTER

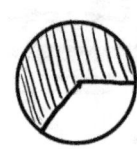
3-7AM

SO AT DAWN, WHEN THE ENERGIES ARE AT THE HIGHEST AS THEY COME INTO OUR BODY, WE REPLENISH OUR BODY'S ENERGIES. AND SO THAT WE DON'T INTERRUPT ITS FLOW, WE DON'T EAT ANYTHING.
THIS IS THE BEST TIME TO MEDITATE.

11AM-2PM

NOON IS LUNCHTIME. IT IS TOO HOT TO MEDITATE. YOU SHOULD JUST EAT AND RELAX.

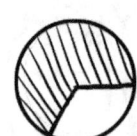
4-7PM

EARLY EVENING OR AFTERNOON IS HARVESTING TIME. FALL IS NOT A GOOD TIME TO PLANT THINGS. RATHER, IT IS TIME FOR DEEP MEDITATIVE INTROSPECTION FOR GATHERING SELF-KNOWLEGE AND WISDOM.

9PM-3AM

DURING PRE-WINTER OR WINTER TIME, WE GO INTO HIBERNATION. IT'S NOT A GOOD TIME TO SOW SEEDS IN THE GROUND BECAUSE THEY WILL NEVER GROW. SO THIS ISN'T A DESIRABLE TIME FOR MEDITATION.

SO, YOU MUST TIME THINGS WISELY. WHEN I TOOK YOU OUT TO DINNER SEVERAL TIMES CLOSE TO MIDNIGHT, OUR BODIES WERE LIKE 70 YRS OLD. I SAY THAT BECAUSE THE BODY IS NOT EQUIPPED TO EAT AT THAT TIME, THOUGH WE PUSH IT THROUGH ANYWAY. THE FOOD ENDS UP SITTING IN THE STOMACH BECAUSE IT ISN'T THE BODY'S TIME TO DIGEST FOOD. NOT ONLY MUST YOU BE AWARE OF WHAT WE EAT, BUT ALSO WHEN WE EAT.

WHEN WE EAT LATE AT NIGHT, WE ARE TELLING OUR BODIES THAT WE DON'T CARE WHAT IT'S DOING IN ITS CYCLE. WE ARE TELLING IT THAT WE ARE GOING TO EAT AND THE BODY MUST DIGEST.

WE CAN DO THAT FROM TIME TO TIME, BUT IF IT BECOMES A CHRONIC HABIT, THE BODY WILL NOT PROCESS THE FOOD. IT WILL SIT THERE ALL NIGHT AND WILL BE DIGESTED THE NEXT DAY. AND PEOPLE WONDER WHY THEY HAVE HEART-BURN AND DIGESTION PROBLEMS AFTER EATING SO LATE AT NIGHT.

"+" AND "−" EQUALS HARMONY

TAKE THE BATTERY AS AN EXAMPLE OF HOW ENERGY WORKS.

OR

DOES NOT WORK. NOTHING SPARKS SO THERE IS NO FLOW OF LIFE.

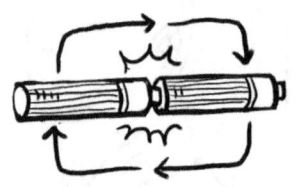

ONLY WHEN YOU HAVE A POSITIVE AND A NEGATIVE CHARGE DOES SOMETHING SPARK AND FLOW.

THIS IS IMPORTANT WHEN YOU THINK ABOUT THE "+" CHARGE AS HEAVEN AND THE "−" CHARGE AS EARTH.

THE HEAVENLY ENERGY BY ITSELF WILL HAVE NOWHERE TO DIRECT ITS INFORMATION.

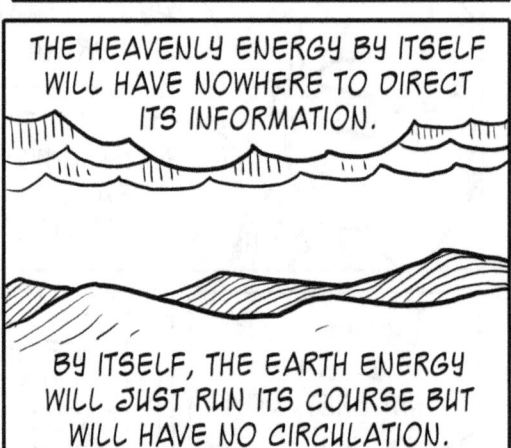

BY ITSELF, THE EARTH ENERGY WILL JUST RUN ITS COURSE BUT WILL HAVE NO CIRCULATION.

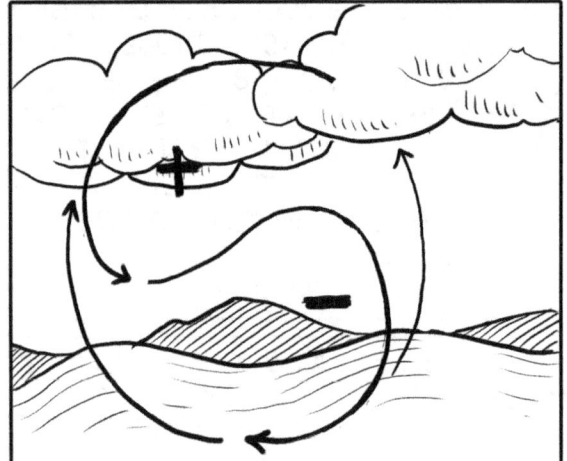

ONLY WHEN THE EARTH'S "−" AND HEAVEN'S "+" ENERGY MEET WILL SOMETHING SPARK AND CREATE HARMONIOUS ENERGY THAT WILL MOVE AND CIRCULATE THROUGHOUT.

IF OUR BODY IS NOT FLOWING AND CIRCULATING PROPERLY, IT IS BECAUSE SOMETHING IS EITHER BROKEN OR MISSING.

AND, A NON-FUNCTIONAL BEING CAN'T FIX ITSELF INTO A FUNCTIONAL BEING.

IF ONE IS WITHOUT THE KNOWLEDGE AND THE WISDOM TO FIX ONESELF, IT IS IMPORTANT TO SEEK OUT PROPER GUIDANCE.

UNFORTUNATELY, NOT EVERYONE FINDS SOMEONE WHO SPECIALIZES IN THEIR PARTICULAR BROKEN PART.

INSIDE OF YOU, THE "+" IS THE CONSCIENCE, AND THE REST IS THE "-" THE LOGICAL MIND.

NEITHER THE "LOGICAL MIND" NOR THE DEEP INNER-CONNECTED KNOWLEDGE OF THE "CONSCIENCE" CAN CREATE HARMONY BY THEMSELVES.

THE TWO PARTS MUST MEET AND SPARK INTO LIFE IN ORDER TO FLOW AND CIRCULATE. THIS ALLOWS THE BODY TO FUNCTION FULLY AND HARMONIOUSLY.

WE HAVE A MYSTERIOUS STRUCTURE. WITHOUT FULLY FUNCTIONING, AND WITHOUT REALLY HAVING THE PLUSES AND THE MINUSES CONNECTED, WE CAN STILL LIVE AND DO WHATEVER WE WANT IN OUR DAY-TO-DAY LIVES.

HOWEVER, WHEN THE "+" AND THE "-" ARE SEPARATED FOR A LONG TIME, WE BECOME NON-FUNCTIONING BEINGS. THOUGH WE ARE LIVING, WE ARE "DEAD".

AS NON-FUNCTIONING BEINGS, WE DON'T KNOW THAT THERE IS ANYTHING TO FIX. OTHERWISE WE WOULD HAVE FIXED IT ALREADY. WE SIMPLY MEET OUR END.

AS NON-FUNCTIONING BEINGS, WE BELIEVE WHATEVER PATH WE ARE ON IS THE CORRECT ONE BECAUSE WE LOOK THROUGH THE NON-FUNCTIONING POINT OF VIEW. EVEN THOUGH FROM THE "FUNCTIONING" VIEW THIS MIGHT BE WRONG, EVERYONE IS GIVEN A CHOICE. WE CAN CHOOSE TO BE FUNCTIONAL OR NON-FUNCTIONAL.

FOR EXAMPLE, YOU THOUGHT YOU HAD A FANTASTIC LIFE. IT LOOKED LIKE YOU HAD EVERYTHING. BUT THOSE THINGS WERE GIVEN TO YOU EITHER BY DESIGN OR LUCK. AND WHEN THE LUCK RAN OUT, WHAT HAPPENED THEN? YOU COULDN'T TELL WHERE THE LUCK BEGAN AND ENDED.

YOU HAD USED UP ALL OF YOUR RESOURCES THAT YOU HAD ENJOYED BEFORE. THEN WHAT HAPPENED?

YOU GOT SICK! YOU ENDED UP BEDRIDDEN WITH UNKNOWN ILLNESSES. IS THAT A GOOD LIFE?

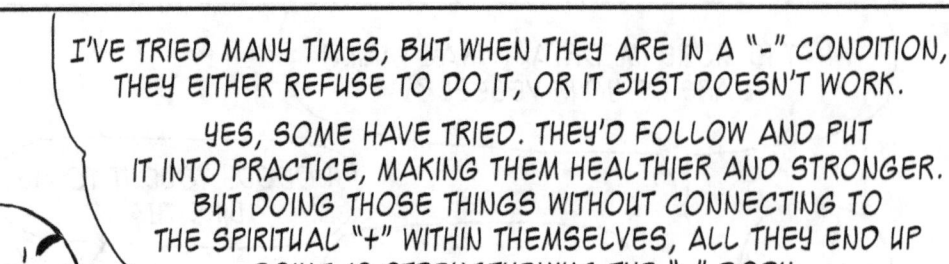

I'VE TRIED MANY TIMES, BUT WHEN THEY ARE IN A "-" CONDITION, THEY EITHER REFUSE TO DO IT, OR IT JUST DOESN'T WORK.

YES, SOME HAVE TRIED. THEY'D FOLLOW AND PUT IT INTO PRACTICE, MAKING THEM HEALTHIER AND STRONGER. BUT DOING THOSE THINGS WITHOUT CONNECTING TO THE SPIRITUAL "+" WITHIN THEMSELVES, ALL THEY END UP DOING IS STRENGTHENING THE "-" BODY.

EVEN THOUGH THEY END UP LOOKING YOUNGER AND HEALTHIER, THERE IS STILL NO SPARK AND FLOW OF ENERGY BETWEEN THE "+" AND THE "-". IT IS NOT A WORKING WHOLE, A UNIFIED MIND AND BODY.

AND THAT'S NOT WHAT I AM HERE TO DO. I AM HERE TO HELP PEOPLE MAKE THE "+" AND "-" CONNECTION.

YEAH, BUT YOU STILL HAVE AN OBLIGATION. MEANING, YOU KNOW HOW THESE THINGS WORK AND SO YOU ARE OBLIGATED TO RELIEVE THEIR SUFFERING.

PERHAPS, THAT IS YOUR JOB.

NOBODY'S GOING TO LISTEN TO ME. I AM NOT A TEACHER TYPE NOR AM I QUALIFIED TO TEACH THIS STUFF.

I DON'T KNOW ABOUT THAT. WE HAVE LOTS OF RESPECTED INTELLECTUALS WHO DO THEIR JOBS WELL. BUT THIS IS NOT ONE OF THEIR SPECIALTIES. MORE THAN SIMPLE KNOWLEDGE, YOU NEED TO KNOW AND UNDERSTAND HOW THE HUMAN BODY AND THE HUMAN MIND WORKS. AND IT SHOULD BE TAUGHT WITH WISDOM AND COMPASSION.

MOST PEOPLE WOULDN'T TAKE UP THIS WORK. THERE IS NO MONEY IN IT, NOR ANY GLORY. HOWEVER, SOMEONE HAS TO DO IT AND EACH ONE OF US IS ENDOWED WITH CERTAIN TALENTS. WE ARE CALLED TO PROVIDE SERVICE TO OTHERS SO THAT OUR EARTHLY LIFE WILL FINALLY SPARK, CONNECT, FLOW AND HARMONIZE.

THE ZEN MASTER EXPLAINED THAT WITHIN ALL OF US EXISTS ALL SENTIENT BEINGS. NOT ONLY DO WE CARRY TRAITS BASED ON OUR DNA, BUT ALSO ALL OTHER TRAITS THAT WE CONSIDER GOOD, BAD, UGLY, CUNNING, MANIPULATIVE, ETC. ONLY WHEN WE ARE AWAKENED TO ALL THESE THINGS, DO THEY DISSOLVE. WHEN CONNEE ASKED WHERE THIS IDEA OF "+"/"-" AND THE MERIDIAN SYSTEM CAME FROM, HE TOLD HER THAT IT WAS MORE THAN A THEORY, AND THAT PEOPLE HAVE BEEN INTERPRETING THESE SYSTEMS THE WRONG WAY.

THIS PARTICULAR THEORY APPEARED IN ANCIENT GOJOSEON. HERMITS LIVING DEEP IN THE FOREST DEVELOPED ANCIENT MEDICINE AND WITH GREAT AWAKENING EYES SAW THE MOVEMENTS OF THE STARS AND THE CHANGING SEASONS. THEY SAW HOW THEY WERE CONNECTED AND THUS ESTABLISHED THE CHUN-MOON (ASTROLOGICAL) THEORY AND THE JI-RI (GEOMANTIC) THEORY.

WHAT THE CHUN-MOON THEORY AND THE JI-RI THEORY DESCRIBE EXISTED FROM THE BEGINNING OF TIME. PEOPLE SIMPLY REALIZED THIS AND IT WAS PUT INTO WRITING.

THEY COULD SEE BENEATH THE SURFACE AND BEGAN TO READ THE LAND, MOUNTAINS, RIVERS, AND SEAS.

THESE PEOPLE ALSO READ THE HUMAN BODY STRUCTURE. THEY SAW IN IT, A SMALL UNIVERSE WHERE ALL THE ORGANS AND MERIDIANS WERE INTERCONNECTED AND PLAYED A ROLE IN HOW IT FUNCTIONED TOGETHER.

THIS IS WHAT WE NOW KNOW AS EASTERN MEDICINE.

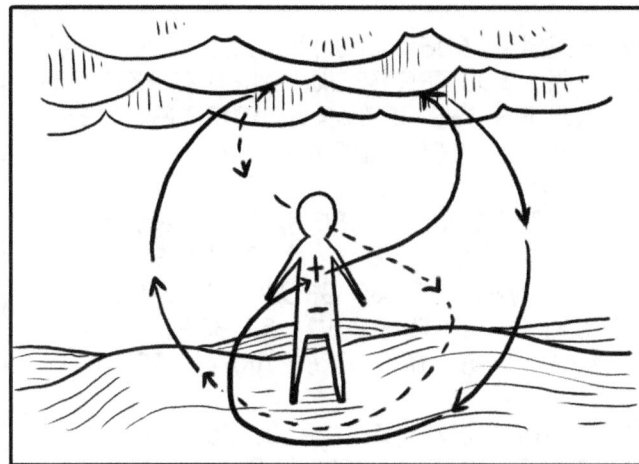

WE HAVE HEAVEN, EARTH, AND ALL THE LIVING THINGS, INCLUDING HUMANS.

THE HEAVEN'S ENERGY AND THE EARTH'S ENERGY CIRCULATE AND FLOW THROUGH US, CONNECTING THE "+" AND THE "-" THROUGH OUR BODY. WHEN CONNECTED CORRECTLY, IT SPARKS, FLOWS, AND HARMONIZE.

ACCORDING TO THE ANCIENT LEGENDS, THE HEAVEN IS "+" AND THE EARTH IS "-". TOGETHER THEY CONTROL ALL THINGS AND CREATE CHANGE. THE "+" AND "-" CARRY DIVINE ENERGY THAT GIVES LIFE AND NURTURE THAT LIFE. THEREFORE, WHEN OUR HUMAN BODIES AND ALL LIVING THINGS HARMONIZE THROUGH THE YIN YANG, MOST ILLNESSES CAN BE FIXED.

THESE ARE THE EXAMPLES OF YIN AND YANG

YIN	MOON	WOMAN	EARTH
YANG	SUN	MAN	HEAVEN

WHENEVER THERE IS "-", THERE IS ALSO A "+". AND ALL LIVING THINGS HAVE THE CAPACITY TO ADJUST THEIR YIN YANG, "+" AND "-".

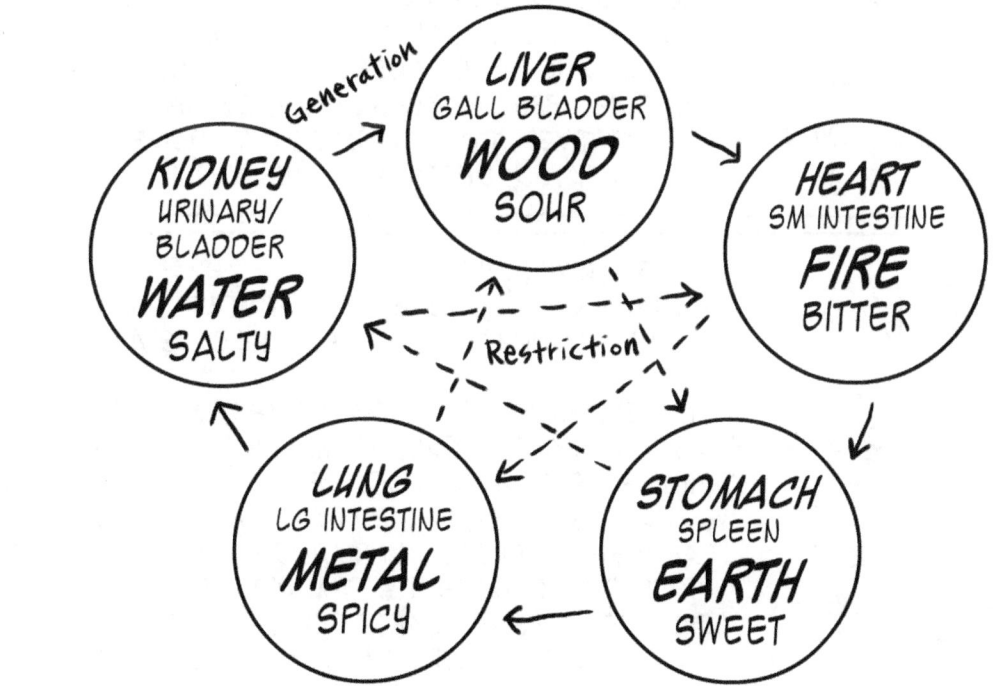

WOOD/LIVER

COLOR: BLUE/GREEN

DIRECTION: EAST (THINK OF LAND AND ROOT, AND ITS UPWARD MOVEMENT.)

LIVER ENERGY IS GENERALLY TALL, SLENDER AND GENTLE. IT SYMBOLIZES SPRING WHEN EVERYTHING COMES TO LIFE. THE SPRING WEATHER IS NICE, WARM, SOFT AND GENTLE.

WHEN THIS PARTICULAR TYPE HAS "+" AND "-" IN HARMONY, IT BECOMES COMPETITIVE AND SEEKS IMPROVEMENT AND GROWTH. THE WOOD NATURE LIKES PRESTIGE AND ARE SOFT, KIND, AND WARM WHEN THEY ARE HARMONIZED.

REPRESENTING LIVER AND GALL BLADDER, IT IS LIKE A SPROUT OF NEW GROWTH. WHEN A PART IS USED, IT WILL GROW BACK, CONSTANTLY REPLENISHING ITSELF. THIS PERSON'S LIVER SYSTEM WILL CONTINUE TO HEAL.

FIRE/HEART

COLOR: RED

DIRECTION: SOUTH

HEART ENERGY SPARKS WHEN "+" AND "-" MEET. IT IS ATTRACTIVE AND BECAUSE PEOPLE LOVE BEAUTIFUL AND GORGEOUS THINGS, PEOPLE FALL MADLY IN LOVE WITH IT.

THE SEASON IS SUMMER, AND LIKE THE SUN/FIRE, IT BRIGHTENS THE SPACE AROUND THEM. BUT ALSO LIKE FIRE, IT DESIRES TO CONSUME AND BURN EVERYTHING AROUND IT, INCLUDING THE PERSON WHO HAS IT.

FIRE ENERGY LOOKS FANTASTIC ON THE OUTSIDE, BUT INSIDE THERE'S A STRUGGLE. IT IS VERY GREEDY AND GOES UP AND UP. TALENTED IN AN ARTISTIC WAY, FIRE NATURE APPEARS PASSIONATE, ENERGETIC, AND INTUITIVE. IT CAN ALSO BE EXPLOSIVE AND OVER-HEATED, DESTROYING THE COOLING SYSTEM.

EARTH/STOMACH

COLOR: YELLOW

DIRECTION: CENTER OR SOUTHWEST

THE STOMACH ENERGY CONNECTS "+" AND "-", AND IN DOING SO, IT CREATES HARMONY AND UNITY, WITH A TENDENCY TO HOLD AND EMBRACE ALL THINGS.

THE STOMACH SITS AT THE CENTER, AND THE FOUR SEASONS CIRCLE AROUND IT, MAKING ALL THINGS GROW. THROUGH ITS CHANGES, COMES THE FINISHED PRODUCT. WE PLANT, GROW, AND THEN HARVEST. THIS IS WHAT THE EARTH ENERGY PERSON PROVIDES, WITH THE HELP OF FOUR OTHER ELEMENTS. IT MAKES THE BODY A BIT DULL BECAUSE THE EARTH ENERGY PUTS EVERYTHING IN, EMBRACING THEM IN A CHAOTIC WAY.

Metal / Lung

COLOR: WHITE

DIRECTION: WEST

THE LUNG ENERGY PULLS WITH "+" AND "−", A STRONG CONTRACTING FORCE. IT IS HARD, FORCEFUL, AND CONTROLLING.

ITS SEASON IS FALL; THEREFORE IT REPRESENTS HARVESTING.

WHEN COMBINED WITH FIRE/HEART ENERGY, IT EXERCISES FAIR JUDGEMENT. WITH THE STRENGTH AND SOFTNESS COEXISTING, IT KNOWS *WHAT TO DO* AND *WHAT NOT TO DO*. IT UNDERSTANDS THE DARK SIDE OF HUMAN NATURE AS WELL AS ITS WEAKNESSES, COMING TO PEOPLE'S AID WHEN NEEDED. PRINCIPLE IS MORE IMPORTANT THAN MONEY FOR THIS ENERGY AND CAN MAKE PEOPLE AROUND THEM NERVOUS.

Water / Kidney

COLOR: BLACK

DIRECTION: NORTH

KIDNEY ENERGY PUSHES AWAY WITH "+" AND "−". ITS TENDENCY IS TO SPREAD OUTWARD, JUST AS WATER FLOWS OVER THE LAND, SOAKING THE EARTH.

ITS SEASON IS WINTER AND IS DAMP, PREPARING FOR THE COMING OF SPRING. IT IS THIS ENERGY THAT ALLOWS THE SPRING LIFE TO GROW.

THIS ENERGY ALSO HOLDS, WHILE REPRESENTING LIFE AND DEATH, AND SOFTENING OF THINGS. IT IS FULL OF KNOWLEDGE, MAKING FOR A SCIENTIFIC MIND THAT RESEARCHES AND IMPROVES, BRINGING POSITIVE IDEAS TO THE TABLE. IT HAS A WAY OF SMOOTHING THINGS OUT IN A SOFTENING WAY. AND BECAUSE IT IS DAMP, IT CAN CREATE MOLD IN THE SYSTEMS IF NOT PROPERLY CIRCULATED.

PEOPLE LIVE A CERTAIN WAY. WHILE SOME MAY HAVE CHOICES, OTHERS MAY NOT. AND WHEN WE ARRIVE AT A CERTAIN POINT IN OUR LIVES, WE ACCEPT IT LIKE THE CHANGING OF THE SEASONS. WHETHER IT'S FUNCTIONAL OR NONFUNCTIONAL, IT CAN APPEAR TO BE THE SAME THING FOR MOST PEOPLE.

YOU ARE BORN, THEN GO TO SCHOOL, GET A JOB, GET MARRIED, BUY A HOUSE AND CAR, AND FINALLY DIE WHEN THE TIME COMES. AND OF COURSE, ILLNESS IS PART OF THE PROCESS IN THAT LIFE. HOWEVER, IT'S NOT IN THE WAY EVERYONE THINKS IT IS.

HOW DO WE HARMONIZE IT, AND BE DIFFERENT? WE DO IT THROUGH "+" AND "-" CONNECTION, TO SPARK, FLOW AND HARMONIZE.

THE FIVE ORGANS

THE UNIQUE COMBINATION OF ENERGIES IN A PERSON DECIDES THE OUTCOME. THE FOLLOWING DESCRIBES THE ENERGIES INDIVIDUALLY AND THE WAY IT MANIFESTS IN A PERSON.

KIDNEY

A PERSON WITH STRONG KIDNEYS HAS EXCESS WATER ENERGY. THE BODY IS BUILT TO HAVE CONTINUOUS WATER ENERGY COMING INTO IT. BECAUSE THEIR BODIES ARE INVADED BY EXCESS WATER ENERGY, THEY WILL LIKELY INVADE OTHER PEOPLE'S SPACES — BE THEY PHYSICAL OR MENTAL. LIKE WATER, THEY WILL FIND A WAY TO FLOW THROUGH AND AROUND OBSTACLES, AND BLINDLY DESIRE TO KEEP GOING.

THIS ALSO HAPPENS IN THE BODY. THE EXCESS WATER ENERGY FLOWS INTO OTHER ORGANS, INTERFERING WITH THE FUNCTION OF THE STOMACH, LUNG, HEART, AND POSSIBLY LIVER. THIS DISRUPTS THE REGULAR FUNCTIONING OF THE BODY SYSTEMS. THIS PARTICULAR ENERGY CAUSES PEOPLE TO BE TALKATIVE, INVASIVE, FEARFUL, MISTRUSTING AND FULL OF DOUBT.

WITH THIS KIND OF BODY, THE PERSON WILL OFTEN HAVE STOMACH PROBLEMS, AND IF FEMALE, WILL HAVE PROBLEMS WITH THE REPRODUCTIVE SYSTEM. TOO MUCH EXCESS KIDNEY ENERGY WILL PUT OUT THE FIRE/HEART, OVER-RUNNING IT, AND CAN CAUSE THE INDIVIDUAL TO DIE IN THEIR SLEEP.

THE WAY TO IMPROVE THIS CONDITION IS TO EAT SWEET AND BITTER FOODS. ALTHOUGH THE WATER ENERGY SEEKS FOODS WITH COLD ELEMENTS TO THEM, ONE MUST AVOID THEM ALL. THE MORE ONE CONSUMES IT, THE SICKER THE BODY WILL BECOME.

HEART

WHEN SOMEONE HAS EXCESS HEART ENERGY, THEY TEND TO BE ATTRACTIVE, LOVE TO GO SHOPPING, AND THEY WANT TO KEEP GOING UP, AND UP AND UP. THEY CANNOT COME DOWN AND GET EASILY DEPRESSED.

WITH EXCESS HEART ENERGY, THEIR KIDNEY SYSTEM IS WEAK. THEY LOOK PRETTIER ON THE OUTSIDE. INSIDE, THEY DEAL WITH NEGATIVITY, DEPRESSION, AND REPRODUCTIVE ORGAN PROBLEMS. THIS TYPE OF PERSON REQUIRES AN AUDIENCE TO LIVE ON. AND WITHOUT THAT AUDIENCE, THEY OFTEN COLLAPSE AND FALL INTO DEPRESSION.

THIS PARTICULAR ENERGY PATTERN WILL ALSO EXPLODE, DUE TO AN ENGINE THAT RUNS TOO HOT AND THE LACK OF "COOLING SYSTEM" (THINK KIDNEYS). THIS BODY STRUCTURE ONLY WANTS TO LIVE IN A SHINY, HIGH-PROFILE PUBLIC LIFESTYLE.

IF THEY WANT TO MAINTAIN THAT KIND OF LIFE AND LIVE LONGER, THEY MUST MAINTAIN THEIR COOLING SYSTEM. THIS IS A MUST. THEY MUST DO THIS BY AVOIDING ALL SWEET AND BITTER FOODS.

LIVER

A PERSON WITH EXCESS LIVER SYSTEM IS GENUINELY KIND, BUT IS IRRESPONSIBLE AND INDECISIVE. IT TAKES A LONG TIME FOR THEM TO MAKE A DECISION, AND THEY ARE NOT ALWAYS CLEAR.

EXCESS LIVER ENERGY WILL WEAKEN THE STOMACH. UNABLE TO BRING THEMSELVES BACK UP, THEY WILL OFTEN FACE DEPRESSION-LIKE SYMPTOMS IF THEY LACK LUNG ENERGY.

FOR PERSONS WITH THIS BODY STRUCTURE TO HAVE CREDIBILITY AND DECISIVENESS, THEY MUST STRENGTHEN LUNG POWER. THIS PERSON IS VERY INTELLECTUAL WHO DOES LOTS OF RESEARCH AND READS A LOT OF BOOKS. THEY TEND TO BE STUBBORN AND TYPICALLY, A KNOW-IT-ALL. WHEN THEY STRENGTHEN THEIR LUNG AND HEART ENERGIES, THEY BECOME VERY NOBLE.

THEY CAN IMPROVE THEIR SITUATION BY EATING BEEF, FISH, LAMB AND SPICY FOODS. HOWEVER, OTHER PROTEINS MUST BE AVOIDED DESPITE THEIR INTELLECT TELLING THEM OTHERWISE. IT DOESN'T KNOW THE BODY'S EXCESSES.

LUNG

SOMEONE WITH GOOD LUNG POWER IS PRINCIPLED, PRECISE, AND OPINIONATED. THOUGH THEY ARE NOT KIND, THEY DO THE MORALLY CORRECT THINGS. AND BECAUSE THEY DO THE RIGHT THING, THEY BELIEVE KINDNESS IS NOT NECESSARY. THEY HAVE A HEROIC MINDSET AND ARE BENEFITTED GREATLY BY FIRE/HEART ENERGY.

EXCESS LUNG WEAKENS THE LIVER, CAUSING THE STOMACH, LIVER, AND HEART TO WORK CONTINUOUSLY. THIS CREATES STRESS ON THE WHOLE SYSTEM, WHICH IN TURN CAUSES THE PERSON TO BECOME IMPATIENT. THOUGH THE LUNG, UNTEMPERED BY THE OTHER ORGANS, IS ABLE TO SEE AND TAKE ACTION, THINGS DON'T HAPPEN THE WAY THEY INTEND.

IN MOST CASES, THIS PARTICULAR PERSON DOES NOT HAVE EMPATHY OR SYMPATHY FOR OTHERS. WE FIND THIS TYPE OFTEN SERVING AS CEO'S AND MILITARY OFFICERS. IF THIS PERSON STRENGTHENS THEIR HEART AND LIVER ENERGY, THEY BECOME LIKE A FINELY HONED SWORD. HOWEVER, WITHOUT THESE ENERGIES, THEY BECOME BLUNT AND ROUGH AROUND THE EDGES, WITH PEOPLE AFRAID TO BE NEAR THEM.

THOUGH THIS ENERGY TYPE LOVES BEEF, FISH, AND ANYTHING SPICY, THEY MUST AVOID EATING THEM IN ORDER TO IMPROVE THEIR SITUATION.

STOMACH

A PERSON WITH EXCESS STOMACH ENERGY IS A COLLECTOR. THEY COLLECT ANYTHING AND EVERYTHING AT ALL COSTS, THROWING AWAY NOTHING. THEY LOVE MONEY AND COLLECT ANYTHING RELATED TO MONEY TO GAIN MORE.

EXCESS STOMACH ENERGY CAUSES ACIDITY AND KIDNEY PROBLEMS WHERE THE KIDNEY DOES NOT FUNCTION PROPERLY. THE CIRCULATION SLOWS DOWN, AND THE BODY TRIES TO HOLD EVERYTHING IN AS MUCH AS POSSIBLE.

TO IMPROVE, THEY NEED TO EAT BITTER FOODS AND FOODS THAT HAVE COLD AND CLEAR ELEMENTAL PROPERTIES.

SHEDDING 54 POUNDS

LIVING AT THE ZEN CENTER UNDER THE ZEN MASTER'S GUIDANCE, CONNEE BECAME MUCH HEALTHIER.

WITH HER BODY CIRCULATING MUCH FASTER THAN BEFORE, SHE LOST FIFTY-FOUR POUNDS IN SIX MONTHS.

"NOW, YOU LOOK LIKE A HEALTHY HUMAN BEING."

"THANK YOU! THIS METHOD IS TOTALLY NEW TO ME, BUT IT CAN REALLY HELP TONS OF PEOPLE LOSE WEIGHT!"

"YES, THERE IS LOT OF OBESITY IN THE U.S. BUT JUST LOSING WEIGHT IS NOT GOING TO WORK. IT HAS TO BE THE WHOLE BODY SINCE OBESITY IS ONLY A FRACTION OF THE REAL PROBLEM."

"WITHOUT TOUCHING THE CORE OF OUR BEING, IT WILL NOT BE A SOLUTION."

"THEN, WHY NOT TEACH THEM THE WHOLE BODY SYSTEM?"

"PEOPLE ONLY WANT TO LOSE THE WEIGHT, NOT THE CAUSES THAT CREATED THE PROBLEM IN THE FIRST PLACE.

WHEN PEOPLE TALK ABOUT THE WHOLE BODY, THEY DON'T REALLY KNOW WHAT THAT MEANS. SO THERE IS VERY LITTLE PROGRESS."

"BEFORE, I DIDN'T KNOW OR EVEN CARE TO KNOW ABOUT ALL THE THINGS I'VE LEARNED HERE. BUT I WANT TO KNOW HOW MY BODY GOT TURNED AROUND IN SUCH A SHORT TIME."

"YOU HELPED GET RID OF A LOT OF THE GARBAGE I HAD, GIVING ME MUCH MORE ENERGY THAN BEFORE. WHAT IS CAUSING THAT?"

"IT'S FROM TAKING THE HOLISTIC APPROACH, COMBINING SUN DOH BREATHING MEDITATIONS, THE HERBS, ZEN PRACTICE AND LIVING THE ZEN LIFE."

"SO EVERYONE AT THE CENTER IS DOING THE ENTIRE COMBINATION AS WELL?"

"YES, AND NO. SOME DO ALL THREE THINGS THAT I MYSELF DO HERE. BUT MOST CHOOSE TO DO ONLY A FEW, LIKE MEDITATION AND ZEN PRACTICE."

"WHY DON'T YOU TEACH THEM ALL OF IT SO THAT THEY CAN BE HEALTHY AS WELL?"

"THAT'S THE LOGICAL MIND. YOU CAN'T FORCE PEOPLE INTO THE SAME SHOE. NOT EVERYONE IS WILLING TO TAKE THE ENTIRE HOLISTIC APPROACH AS YOU DID.

THEIR NEEDS AND DESIRES ARE DIFFERENT."

"TO BE IN THE ZEN CENTER MEANS WE SHARE A SINGLE COMMON GOAL, DOESN'T IT?"

"EVERYONE IS AT A DIFFERENT PHASE IN THEIR LIVES. ONCE THEY ARE DONE WITH ONE, THEY CAN MOVE ON TO THE NEXT. IT IS LIKE STARTING IN ELEMENTARY SCHOOL AND GRADUATING INTO COLLEGE. WHILE SOME STAY IN THE "KINDERGARTEN" PHASE, OTHERS DESIRE TO MOVE FORWARD TOWARD INDEPENDENCE.

HAVING AWARENESS IS VERY IMPORTANT. WITH IT, YOU KNOW WHAT TO DO AND WHEN TO MOVE ON. YOU SEE THE SIGNS. HOWEVER, MANY RELY ON LOGIC OR THEIR TEACHERS TO DIRECT THEM REGARDING WHAT TO DO AND WHEN TO GO."

 SELF-AWARENESS IS VERY IMPORTANT. WHEN YOU ARE AWARE FROM WITHIN, THE WISDOM PART, YOUR ACTIONS WILL NOT HAVE A NEGATIVE OUTCOME. A TEACHER'S JOB IS NOT TO TELL THE STUDENTS WHAT TO DO OR HOW TO LIVE THEIR LIVES. WHEN YOU ARE SELF-AWARE, YOU KNOW WHAT YOU WANT, AND WHAT YOU NEED TO DO. AND YOU SIMPLY DO IT.

THOUGH YOUR TEACHER COULD TELL YOU WHETHER SOMETHING IS WRONG OR RIGHT, IT ISN'T THEIR JOB TO EXPLAIN TO YOU HOW TO LIVE YOUR LIFE. THEY CAN PROVIDE YOU WITH GUIDELINES, BUT SHOULDN'T TAKE YOU THROUGH EACH STEP OF THE WAY. WHEN YOU HAVE SELF-AWARENESS, YOU SET YOUR LIFE'S COURSE ON YOUR OWN.

 OKAY, I THINK I GOT IT! HOW ABOUT GIVING ALL YOUR STUDENTS THE SAME TEACHINGS YOU GAVE ME?

I DID. I POURED ALL I HAD TO GIVE THEM THE EXPERIENCE THAT I HAD. THEY APPRECIATED IT, MARVELING AND DREAMING ABOUT IT. BUT MOST WERE CONTENT TO JUST LICK THE OUTSIDE OF THE FRUIT INSTEAD OF TAKING A BITE AND TASTING IT FOR THEMSELVES TO KNOW WHAT IT WAS.

THEY WERE JUST HAPPY TO GET TO THAT POINT. BUT IT WON'T BE REAL UNTIL THEY ACTUALLY EAT THE FRUIT. UNTIL THEN, THEY LIVE IN THEIR DREAMS. THEY HAVE CHOSEN TO BE WHERE THEY ARE, AND MAY NEED TO BE THERE FOR THE TIME BEING. AND THAT TIME MAY BE A SECOND OR MANY LIFE-TIMES BEFORE THEY REALIZE IT.

 I SEE... I'VE TESTED OVER 80 PERCENT OF THE HERB FORMULAS, SEEING HOW THEY AFFECTED DIFFERENT ORGANS AS THEY WERE PROCESSED IN THE BODY. COULDN'T THOSE WHO ARE DILIGENTLY PRACTICING BENEFIT FROM THESE FORMULAS?

FOR EXAMPLE, FORMULA 2 CAN JUMP START MARCUS'S PRACTICE, ALLOWING HIM TO MEET HIS GOALS QUICKLY.

 YES, THAT WOULD HELP. HOWEVER, MARCUS BELIEVES THAT IF HE IS DETERMINED ENOUGH, HE CAN GET THERE EVEN WITH A BROKEN WHEEL.

FUNCTIONS

THE ZEN MASTER NOT ONLY TAUGHT CONNEE AT THE ZEN CENTER, HE ALSO TAUGHT HER ON THEIR MORNING AND EVENING WALKS, AFTER PRACTICE AT LOCAL PARKS, DRIVES, AND WHILE THEY ATE. HE NEVER LET GO, AS IF NO TIME WAS TO BE WASTED.

IF YOU LOOK AROUND, YOU WILL SEE THAT THERE ARE A GREAT MANY DIFFERENT LIVES COEXISTING UNDER AND AROUND TREES.

I DIDN'T NOTICE THEM BEFORE. I HAD NEITHER THE TIME NOR THE MIND TO LOOK BEYOND MY OWN ISSUES.

PEOPLE ARE TOO BUSY. THEY LIVE AS MACHINES UNDER AN AUTOMATED SYSTEM THAT DOESN'T LET THEM TAKE TIME FOR THEMSELVES OR OTHERS.

ZEN IS ABOUT BEING AWARE OF THE NOW, THIS EXACT MOMENT.

I THOUGHT I WAS AWARE AT ALL TIMES.

MANY ZEN PRACTITIONERS CLAIM THEY ARE. BUT JUST BECAUSE THEY'VE BEEN PRACTICING DOESN'T MEAN THAT THEY ARE AWARE OF THE PRESENT MOMENT.

HOW DO I MAKE SURE THAT I AM NOT ASSUMING ANYTHING, AND THAT I AM ACTUALLY PRESENT?

REST YOUR BUSY MIND, AND DON'T FOLLOW YOUR THOUGHTS. SIMPLY WATCH THOSE THOUGHTS LIKE YOU DO WITH T.V. WHEN YOU WATCH T.V., YOU ARE NOT ATTACHED TO THE SHOW. YOU MIGHT CONNECT EMOTIONALLY HERE AND THERE, BUT THEY AREN'T YOUR EMOTIONS.

MENDING OLD WOUNDS

AS CONNEE GREW IN HER PRACTICE AND BECAME HEALTHIER, SHE REALIZED THAT SHE HAD SAID SOME HARSH WORDS TO HER EX-HUSBAND DAVID AT THE END OF THEIR MARRIAGE. THE WORDS HAD BEEN WRONG, AND IT BOTHERED HER. NO MATTER HOW MUCH PAIN HE HAD CAUSED HER, SHE HAD STILL ACTED OUT FROM A PLACE OF ANGER AND DISHARMONY. SHE WENT TO THE ZEN MASTER AND RECEIVED PERMISSION TO GO TO SEATTLE AND SPEAK WITH DAVID.

SHE MET HIM AT THE BEACH THEY USED TO GO TO. DAVID WAS SURPRISED AND WONDERED AT THE URGENCY TO MEET WITH HIM.

DAVID, THANK YOU FOR MEETING ME HERE.

WOW, YOU LOOK JUST LIKE WHEN I FIRST MET YOU, FIT AND BEAUTIFUL.

MY MOM TOLD ME YOU HAD HEALTH ISSUES AND HAD GAINED WEIGHT. YOU DON'T LOOK SICK AT ALL. IS EVERYTHING OKAY?

I AM HERE TO APOLOGIZE FOR ALL THE WRONGS I DID TO YOU.

!

I USED TO THINK THAT MOST OF OUR PROBLEMS STEMMED FROM YOU. BUT AS MY BODY RECOVERED AND MY PRACTICE CONTINUED, I REALIZED IT HAD BEEN MOSTLY MY FAULT. I WAS NOT IN HARMONY.

I AM SO SORRY FOR ALL THOSE YEARS I'VE BLAMED YOU FOR EVERYTHING.

CONNEE, YOU CAME ALL THE WAY FROM SAN FRANCISCO TO TELL ME THIS?

I AM HONORED.

I WANTED TO TELL YOU IN PERSON, TO PROVE MY SINCERITY AND IN HOPES THAT THIS WILL EASE SOME OF THE HURT I'VE CAUSED.

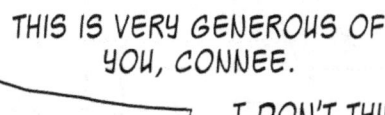

"THIS IS VERY GENEROUS OF YOU, CONNEE.

I DON'T THINK I CAN DO WHAT YOU ARE DOING RIGHT NOW. OTHERWISE I'D BE SPENDING THE REST OF MY LIFE LOOKING FOR PEOPLE TO CORRECT ALL THE WRONGS I'VE DONE.

DO YOU KNOW WHAT I WAS THINKING WHEN YOU ASKED ME TO MEET YOU?"

"DID YOU THINK THAT I HAD WANTED MY SHARE OF THE ASSETS?"

"YES. I THOUGHT YOU WERE HERE TO CLAIM YOUR FAIR SHARE OF THE ASSETS. YOU HAD CHOSEN TO WALK AWAY FROM IT, BUT I SHOULD HAVE STILL GIVEN YOU YOUR SHARE.

I WASN'T A GOOD PERSON AND IT'S BEEN ON MY CONSCIENCE - WHICH I'VE BEEN IGNORING ALL THIS TIME."

"HAHAHA! WHAT A SILLY THOUGHT.

EVEN WITH HAVING MORE THAN ENOUGH, MONEY IS STILL A VERY IMPORTANT PART OF YOU, HUH? SORRY TO DISAPPOINT YOU.

HA HA HA! THAT'S SUCH AN UNNECESSARY WORRY FOR YOU, DAVID."

"I GUESS. I COULDN'T THINK OF ANY OTHER REASON WHY YOU'D WANT TO SEE ME."

"AS I PRACTICE, SOME THINGS COME TO THE SURFACE AND ARE RELEASED, WHILE OTHERS ARE RENEWED.

YOU SAVED MY LIFE ONCE WITHOUT REALIZING IT. I THANK YOU FOR THAT. I COULDN'T TAKE MONEY FROM SOMEONE WHO SAVED MY LIFE."

"I DIDN'T SAVE YOU. IT WAS JUST BUDDHA'S WAY OF GIVING ME THE CHANCE TO MEET YOU.

SO, IN MY MIND, I DIDN'T PLAY FAIR WITH YOU CONCERNING THE ASSETS. MAYBE THAT'S WHY I'VE BEEN SO ANXIOUS ALL THIS TIME. IT'S STUPID. I ALREADY HAVE MORE THAN ENOUGH."

"YOU HAVE THE MONEY, AND I HAVE THE FREEDOM.

I AM REALLY GLAD WE GOT TO HAVE THIS MEETING."

THE ZEN MASTER WHO SWEPT AND POLISHED

THE ZEN MASTER TOLD CONNEE A STORY. THERE ONCE WAS A MAN WHO WENT TO ONE OF THE GREAT ZEN MASTERS OF THAT TIME AND ASKED IF HE COULD BE HIS STUDENT. THE GREAT ZEN MASTER AGREED AND TOLD THIS MAN TO ASSIST THE COOK AND SWEEP AROUND THE MONASTERY. THE MAN QUIETLY DID HIS JOB FOR TWO YEARS, WITHOUT A SINGLE COMPLAINT.

AT THE END OF THOSE TWO YEARS, THE MAN APPROACHED THE GREAT ZEN MASTER.

MASTER, I'VE BEEN HERE TWO YEARS, DOING WHAT YOU'VE TOLD ME. NOW, I'D LIKE TO STUDY ZEN ALONG WITH THE OTHERS IN THE ZEN HALL. I WISH TO BECOME A ZEN MASTER SOMEDAY.

KEEP SWEEPING AND POLISHING.

THE GREAT ZEN MASTER SPOKE ONLY THOSE WORDS. THE MAN WENT BACK TO HIS SWEEPING AND POLISHING. THOUGH HE'D ASK THE GREAT ZEN MASTER ONCE EVERY YEAR TO ALLOW HIM TO JOIN THE OTHERS IN LEARNING ZEN, HE WAS ALWAYS GIVEN THE SAME ANSWER: "SWEEP AND POLISH."

EVENTUALLY, THE MAN THOUGHT ABOUT LEAVING THE MONASTERY BECAUSE HE HAD LEARNED NOTHING. ALL HE EVER DID WAS SWEEP AND ASSIST IN COOKING. THAT WASN'T WHY HE HAD COME TO THE MONASTERY. INSIDE, HE RESENTED THE FIVE WASTED YEARS, BUT DECIDED TO WAIT A LITTLE MORE. AFTER ALL, FIVE YEARS WAS A LONG TIME TO HAVE NOTHING TO SHOW FOR IT.

BECAUSE THIS GREAT ZEN MASTER HAD SUCH A REPUTATION, THERE WERE MANY ZEN STUDENTS AT THE MONASTERY. THE MAN OVERHEARD SOME OF THEM DISCUSSING HOW THE GREAT ZEN MASTER WAS INVITED TO ADDRESS OVER 200 ZEN MASTERS, ABBOTS, STUDENTS AND SCHOLARS OF ZEN MIND. UNFORTUNATELY, THE GREAT ZEN MASTER COULD NOT ATTEND BECAUSE HE HAD A PREVIOUS COMMITMENT. THE STUDENTS WONDERED WHO WOULD GIVE THE TALK IN HIS STEAD.

THE MAN TRIED TO THINK OF SOMETHING WHILE HE GOT READY, WHILE HE WAS IN THE CAR, AND WHILE HE WALKED INTO THE BUILDING.

THE GREAT ZEN MASTER WAS TRYING TO TEACH HIM SOMETHING, BUT PERHAPS HIS MENTOR WAS BECOMING SENILE. THE MAN COULD NOT UNDERSTAND THIS SITUATION.

MANY BIG NAMES FROM THE ZEN WORLD WOULD ATTEND THIS EVENT. HE WAS THE ONLY ONE WHO HAD NEVER GONE TO ZEN RETREATS OR SCHOOLS. WHAT COULD HE POSSIBLY SAY TO THEM? HE HAD NO IDEA.

THE EVENT BEGAN. WHEN THE TIME CAME FOR THE DHARMA TALK, THE HOST GAVE A REGRETFUL EXPLANATION AS TO WHY THE GREAT ZEN MASTER COULDN'T GIVE THE SPEECH AND EXPLAINED THAT ONE OF HIS STUDENTS WHO HAD STUDIED UNDER HIM FOR FIVE YEARS WOULD SPEAK INSTEAD. THE CROWD APPLAUDED AND WAITED FOR THE MAN TO APPROACH THE PODIUM.

AS THE MAN WALKED ONTO THE STAGE, HIS MIND WAS STILL A BLANK. WHY HAD HIS TEACHER SENT HIM HERE? THE MAN BOWED FROM THE STAGE IN FRONT OF 200 GUESTS AND STOOD SILENTLY. THE ONLY INSTRUCTION THE MAN EVER RECEIVED FROM HIS TEACHER WAS SIMPLY "SWEEP AND POLISH!". AND THAT WAS ALL HE HAD DONE THESE FIVE YEARS. SO IN A LOUD VOICE, HE SAID –

SWEEP AND POLISH!

SWEEP AND POLISH EVERYDAY!

THE MAN SPOKE THESE WORDS WITH ALL THE CONVICTION HE HAD, FOR THAT WAS ALL HE COULD SAY. HE STOOD THERE QUIETLY AFTER THAT. SUDDENLY, ALL THE ZEN PRACTITIONERS AND ZEN MASTERS ROSE TO GIVE THE MAN A STANDING OVATION.

HE LED AND TAUGHT THE NEXT GENERATION OF THE ZEN WORLD AFTER THAT. AND THAT IS THE END OF THE STORY.

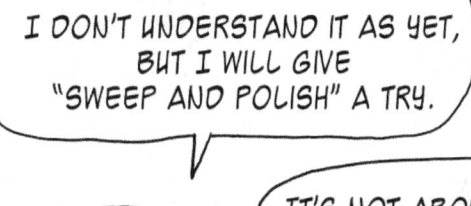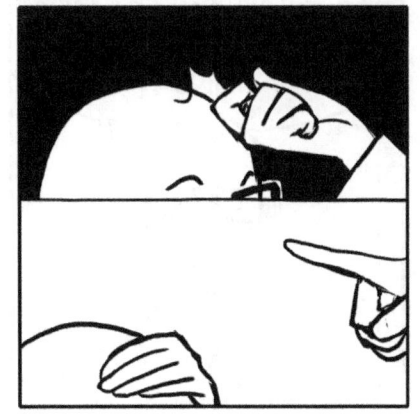

KOAN*

*A riddle that Zen Buddhists use during meditation to help them unravel greater truths about the world and about themselves.

KOAN 2

The following week, the Zen master gave Connee another koan. She replied that it also was not hers.

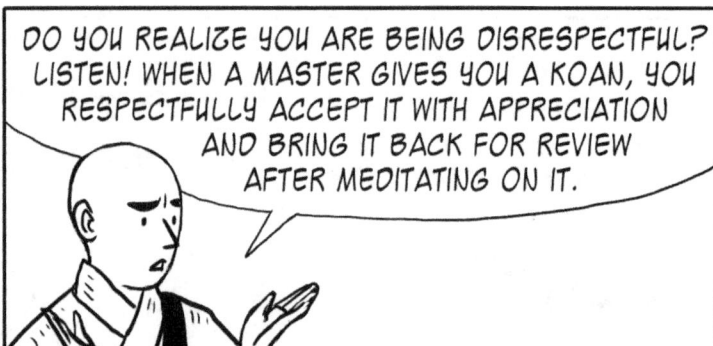

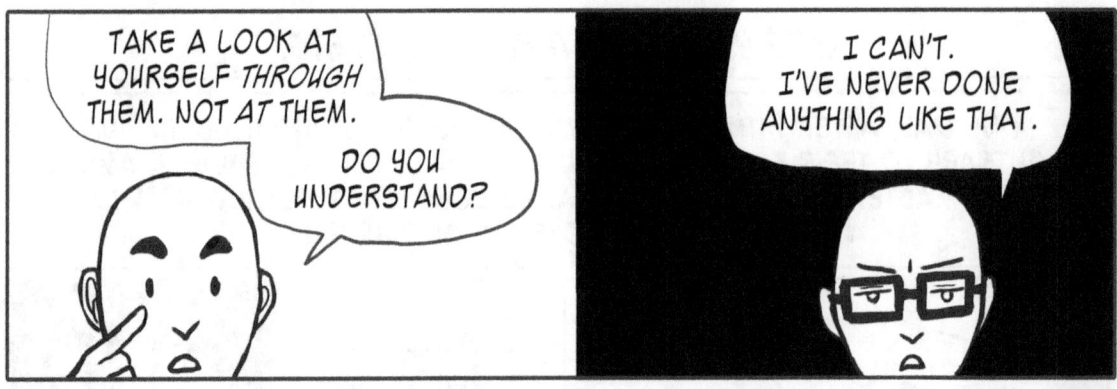

THE ZEN MASTER STAYED SILENT AS CONNEE STRUGGLED WITH HER RIGHTEOUS INDIGNATION. SHE DIDN'T KNOW WHAT TO DO WITH IT AND COULDN'T LET GO.

THE ZEN MASTER SUGGESTED THAT SHE GIVE IT A TRY, AND SEE WHY SHE WAS SO JUDGMENTAL AND ANGRY AT THEM.

DESPITE THE RESISTANCE AND DISCOMFORT, SHE GAVE IT A TRY. SHE SOON FELT SUCH RESISTANCE WITHIN HERSELF THAT SHE WANTED TO CALL IT QUITS. SHE WANTED TO JUST WALK AWAY FROM THIS SELF-INQUIRY AND SAY SOMETHING TO THE ZEN MASTER, BUT HE WAS OFF IN A DISTANT MEDITATIVE STATE.

SHE HAD NO CHOICE BUT TO AGAIN TURN INWARD IN SILENCE.

GOLDEN GATE BRIDGE

THE ZEN MASTER HAD BEEN TRYING TO GET THROUGH TO CONNEE FOR WEEKS. FOR SOME REASON, NOTHING WAS GETTING THROUGH TO HER. CONNEE, FOR HER PART, DIDN'T UNDERSTAND WHAT HE WAS TRYING TO TEACH OR CONVEY TO HER. TENSION AND CONFUSION BETWEEN THEM GREW PALPABLE AS THE ZEN MASTER'S IMPATIENCE INCREASED.

WHY ARE YOU HERE?

I AM HERE TO LEARN, OF COURSE.

THEN WHY AREN'T YOU LEARNING?

I AM DOING EVERYTHING YOU TOLD ME TO DO.

NOT EVERYTHING. AT THE BEGINNING, YOU WERE SICK. NOW YOU ARE MUCH BETTER, HAVING BECOME A FUNCTIONAL BEING. AND YET YOU'RE NOT LEARNING ANYTHING, AS IF YOU'VE FORGOTTEN.

I ASSURE YOU THAT I AM VERY MUCH ON IT.

I DON'T SEE IT. ARE YOU CONTENT WITH WHERE YOU ARE NOW?

NO, I AM NOT.

THEN PROVE IT.

CONNEE ASKED HOW SHE'D BE ABLE TO PROVE IT, AS SHE WAS WILLING TO DO ANYTHING HE ASKED. SHE HAD COMPLETE FAITH IN HIM. WHEN THE ZEN MASTER ASKED HER IF SHE'D BE WILLING TO JUMP OFF THE GOLDEN GATE BRIDGE, SHE REPLIED YES WITHOUT HESITATION. THE ZEN MASTER TOOK IT UP A NOTCH BY SAYING THAT SHE HAD TO MAKE IT CLEAN SINCE HE DIDN'T WANT TO BE BLAMED FOR HER DEATH. SHE AGREED. ASKED WHEN CONNEE WAS GOING TO JUMP, SHE REPLIED THAT SHE'D JUMP WHEN HE TOLD HER TO DO SO.

WITH THIS KIND OF TRUST AND DETERMINATION, WHY AREN'T YOU LETTING THINGS GO?

YOU HAVE NOT GIVEN ME SOMETHING TO REPLACE IT WITH.

THE ZEN MASTER CHUCKLED AND TOLD CONNEE THAT HER THOUGHTS WERE LOPSIDED. HE SAID THAT SHE HAD TO FIRST MAKE ROOM WITHIN HERSELF BY LETTING GO OF ALL HER INNER BAGGAGE, OTHERWISE NOTHING COULD GO IN. CONNEE STILL RESISTED, UNWILLING TO LET IT ALL GO.

NO WONDER NOTHING HAS BEEN WORKING FOR A WHILE. YOU HAVE CLUNG TO EVERYTHING, SO HOW CAN ANYTHING GO IN TO REPLACE THAT "I" OF YOURS? YOUR STORAGE IS COMPLETELY FULL.

ISN'T IT A TEACHER'S JOB TO BREAK THROUGH ALL THAT?

HA HA HA. A TEACHER'S JOB IS NOT TO MAKE OR BREAK YOU. IT IS TO MERELY SHOW YOU THE WAY. WHETHER TO FOLLOW OR NOT IS UP TO THE STUDENT.

CONNEE WAS CRESTFALLEN THAT THE ZEN MASTER, AS AN ENLIGHTENED BEING, COULDN'T GET RID OF HER INNER BAGGAGE FOR HER. WHEN THE ZEN MASTER STERNLY TOLD HER TO GET RID OF ALL THAT WAS HINDERING HER JOURNEY, CONNEE AGAIN DEMANDED A REPLACEMENT.

ENJOY EMPTYING YOUR STORAGE RIGHT NOW.

I'VE GOT TO HAVE SOMETHING TO REPLACE IT WITH. OTHERWISE, SOMETHING ELSE COULD COME IN TO FILL THAT EMPTY SPACE. AND THAT SPACE IS RESERVED ONLY FOR TRUE DHARMA.

I'VE NEVER MET ANYONE SO DIFFICULT, STUBBORN, AND DEMANDING AS YOU. DO YOU SEE ANYONE HERE WHO'S AS DEMANDING AND IMPAIRED AS YOU?

THE BLOOD SERMON - STARS AND BRUISES

AROUND 3AM, A KNOCK RAPPED ON CONNEE'S DOOR. IN THE GLOOM OF DAWN, CONNEE HEARD THE ZEN MASTER'S VOICE FROM OUTSIDE, TELLING HER TO COME TO HIS OFFICE. AFTER QUICKLY WASHING HER FACE TO WAKE HERSELF UP, CONNEE OBEYED.

HE COMMANDED CONNEE TO SIT AND TOLD HER THAT SHE WAS GOING TO LEARN ABOUT THE BODHIDHARMA. HE EXPLAINED WHO THIS PERSON WAS AND WHAT HE HAD ACCOMPLISHED. THEN HE OPENED UP A VERY OLD BOOK.

THE ZEN MASTER WENT OVER ONLY SMALL SECTIONS OF THE BOOK AT A TIME AND FORBADE CONNEE TO HAVE THE BOOK. NEVERTHELESS, CONNEE WAS ENTHRALLED BY THE MEANING BEHIND THE TEXTS. SHE ASKED THE ZEN MASTER MANY QUESTIONS ON THE FOLLOWING DAYS, AND SHE COULDN'T WAIT FOR THE NEXT CLASS.

THE ZEN MASTER NOTICED CONNEE'S OBVIOUS EXCITEMENT AND COMMENTED THAT SHE HAD NEVER SHOWN SUCH ENTHUSIASM.

THE SECOND BLOW CAME BEFORE SHE COULD FINISH THE SENTENCE. AGAIN ON THE FLOOR, CONNEE'S HEAD REELED IN PAIN AND CONFUSION. SHE STRUGGLED TO BRING HERSELF TO CONSCIOUSNESS AS THE ZEN MASTER DEMANDED AGAIN THAT SHE REPEAT WHAT SHE WAS ABOUT TO SAY, HIS VOICE CARRYING EVEN DEEPER ANGER. SHE KEPT QUIET.

WHEN BLOOD RAN THROUGH HER FINGERS ON TO THE FLOOR, THE ZEN MASTER QUIETLY ATTENDED TO THE WOUND. HE TILTED HER HEAD AND COMPRESSED THE BLEEDING UNTIL IT HAD STOPPED. HE THEN TOLD TO GO WASH HER FACE. CONNEE NOTICED THAT THERE WAS NO ANGER IN HIS VOICE.

WITH HER BODY SHAKEN AND HER RIGHT EYE SWOLLEN SHUT, CONNEE STUMBLED TO THE BATHROOM. SHE WASHED HER FACE, SHOCKED TO SEE THE DAMAGE. SHE HARDLY RECOGNIZED THE FACE AS HER OWN. THOUGHTS CAME CRASHING THROUGH HER HEAD, WITH THE BIGGEST ONE BEING: WHY?

WHEN CONNEE RETURNED TO THE ZEN MASTER'S OFFICE, SHE SAW HIM WAITING, WITH ALL TRACES OF BLOOD WIPED OFF THE FLOOR. WHEN SHE SAT DOWN, HE ASKED HER AGAIN TO REPEAT WHAT SHE WAS ABOUT TO SAY.

CONNEE REALIZED THAT HE WASN'T GOING TO LET THIS GO. AT THAT MOMENT, ALL SHE COULD SEE WAS AN ANGRY TEACHER WHO WAS REFUSING TO BACK DOWN. HE WAS WITHOUT COMPASSION, NOT EVEN ASKING IF SHE WAS OKAY, OR AT LEAST OFFERING AN EXPLANATION OR AN APOLOGY. WITH SOME EFFORT CONNEE BRUSHED OFF THESE THOUGHTS AND TRIED TO FOCUS ON THE PRESENT.

ALL SHE HAD DONE WAS TO TELL THE TRUTH AND TRY TO REVEAL A PAST EXPERIENCE. AND WHY WAS SHE HIT A SECOND TIME? WHATEVER THE REASON, CONNEE WASN'T GOING TO SAY IT ANYMORE. NOT AT THAT PRICE.

   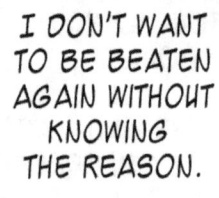   

EVERYONE THEY PASSED STARED. THE WAITRESS TAKING THEIR ORDER WAS VISIBLY SHOCKED AT CONNEE'S FACE, BUT SHE SAID NOTHING ABOUT IT. CONNEE COULD SEE THE COOKS AND KITCHEN HELPERS PEEKING OUT TO GET A LOOK AT THEM, ALONG WITH THE REST OF THE DINERS BUT NO ONE SAID ANYTHING. CONNEE AND THE ZEN MASTER SIMPLY ATE THEIR BREAKFAST AND CARRIED ON AS IF NOTHING HAD HAPPENED.

THEY BOTH LAUGHED. AND WHEN THEY RETURNED TO THE CENTER, EVERYONE WAS STUNNED BY CONNEE'S FACE. NO ONE ASKED QUESTIONS AND NEITHER CONNEE NOR THE ZEN MASTER OFFERED ANY EXPLANATIONS. THEY SIMPLY CARRIED ON AS IF NOTHING HAD HAPPENED. THE INCIDENT WAS NEVER DISCUSSED BETWEEN THEM.

AFTER THAT MORNING, THERE WAS SOMETHING IN CONNEE THAT CREATED PEACE, CONFIDENCE AND FREEDOM THAT WASN'T THERE BEFORE. SHE WAS NO LONGER THE SAME PERSON FROM THE PREVIOUS DAY. EVEN THE ZEN MASTER TREATED HER DIFFERENTLY AFTER THAT.

SOME TIME LATER AT THE MOUNT JI-RI TRAINING CENTER, CONNEE WOULD EXPERIENCE THINGS SIMILAR TO WHAT THE ZEN MASTER HAD SO PAINFULLY TAUGHT HER NOT TO REVEAL. THE NEXT LINES OF THE BOOK HAD SHOWN THAT HIS VIOLENT LESSON WAS FOR HER PROTECTION—THAT THERE WERE THINGS SHE MUST KEEP SECRET AND GUARD CLOSELY. SHE RECALLED THE SPINNING STARS AND THE COLORS RED, BLUE, YELLOW, BLACK AND PURPLE.

SHE WOULD KEEP TO HERSELF THESE VITAL EXPERIENCES EVEN AS SHE LATER RETURNED TO THE ZEN MASTER TO THANK HIM. THE ZEN MASTER WOULD TELL HER THAT IT HAD TAKEN THIRTY YEARS FOR HIM TO GET WHAT CONNEE HAD ACHIEVED IN SUCH A SHORT TIME. SHE'D ONLY REPLY WITH A SMILE.

THE ENERGIES AT BIRTH

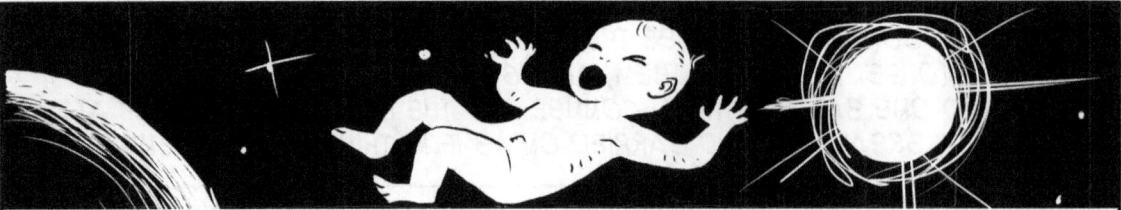

AT BIRTH, WHEN A CHILD COMES OUT OF THE MOTHER'S WOMB, AND THE UMBILICAL CORD IS CUT, THE CHILD TAKES ITS FIRST BREATH. THE CHILD EITHER CRIES OR YAWNS, TAKING IN WHATEVER ENERGY THAT THE UNIVERSE PROVIDES AT THAT TIME. THAT DETERMINES THE STRENGTH OF EACH OF ITS ORGANS AND THE ORGANS' ENERGY SYSTEMS. IT WILL DECIDE WHETHER THE CHILD WILL HAVE STRONG LUNGS, HEART, LIVER, KIDNEYS AND OTHER CONNECTING ORGANS. AND THE STRENGTH OF THESE ORGANS WILL DETERMINE HOW THE PHYSICAL BODY FUNCTIONS.

TO MAKE CLEAR, THIS IS ONLY TALKING ABOUT THE PHYSICAL PART. HOWEVER, THE TRUE SELF WORKS THROUGH THIS PHYSICAL PART, SO IT'S CRUCIAL THAT ONE UNDERSTANDS WHAT ITS FUNCTIONS ARE AND KNOW HOW TO INTERPRET THEM. WHEN THE PHYSICAL PART IS IN DISHARMONY AND ISN'T INTERPRETED CORRECTLY, THE MESSAGE IS EITHER LEFT UNANSWERED OR MISUNDERSTOOD.

IT'S RARE FOR ONE TO BE BORN WITH A HARMONIZED BODY ENERGY STRUCTURE. FOR MOST OF US, WE'RE NOT HARMONIZED, AND WE HAVE TO LIVE ACCORDING TO THE WAY OUR ORGANS ARE STRUCTURED. AND WITHOUT FAIL, WE WILL LIVE OUR LIVES EXACTLY ACCORDING TO THE WAY WE ARE BUILT. THERE IS A SMALL PORTION OF THE POPULATION WHO ARE NOT AFFECTED AS MUCH BY THEIR CONDITION, BUT MOST OF US LIVE OUT OUR NONHARMONIZED SYSTEM.

TO BALANCE THE BODY, WE MUST FEED THE PARTS THAT ARE THE WEAKEST TO HELP CREATE BALANCE WITHIN. HOWEVER, IF A PERSON HAS A SPECIFIC TASK IN THEIR LIFE THAT MUST BE ACCOMPLISHED AND REQUIRES THAT PARTICULAR ENERGY, THEN THEY SHOULDN'T CHANGE ANYTHING UNTIL THE TASK IS DONE. THEY CAN HARMONIZE AFTERWARDS. OFTEN THOUGH, WE CONTINUE IN OUR OLD LIFESTYLE EVEN THOUGH WE HAVE CHANGED. WE MUST BE AWARE OF THE DIFFERENT ROLES EACH ORGAN PLAYS IN OUR LIVES.

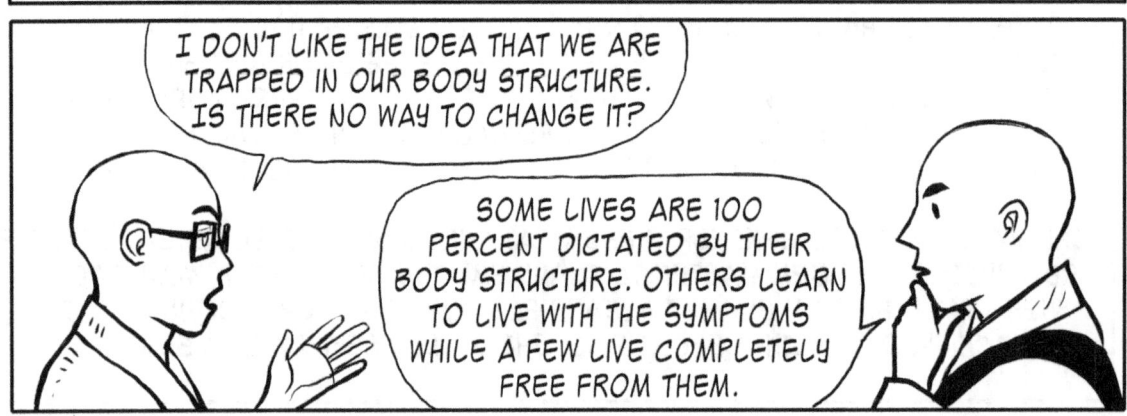

"I DON'T LIKE THE IDEA THAT WE ARE TRAPPED IN OUR BODY STRUCTURE. IS THERE NO WAY TO CHANGE IT?"

"SOME LIVES ARE 100 PERCENT DICTATED BY THEIR BODY STRUCTURE. OTHERS LEARN TO LIVE WITH THE SYMPTOMS WHILE A FEW LIVE COMPLETELY FREE FROM THEM."

"I KNOW ONLY A VERY FEW WHO ARE NOT AFFECTED BY THEIR BODY STRUCTURE. THEY ARE USUALLY THE ONES WHO HAVE ACHIEVED A HIGHER LEVEL IN THEIR SPIRITUAL PRACTICE."

"MOSTLY, I WOULD SAY 99.99 PERCENT OF THE POPULATION IS VERY MUCH AFFECTED BY THEIR BODY WITHOUT REALIZING WHAT'S REALLY HAPPENING. WE OFTEN THINK WE'RE SMART AND SOPHISTICATED, AND HAVE EVERYTHING FIGURED OUT."

"YOU HAVE MANY DISCIPLES LIVING IN THIS CENTER."

"HOW MANY ARE STILL AFFECTED AND HOW MANY ARE NOT?"

"ALL ARE AFFECTED. NONE ARE FREE FROM IT."

THE ZEN MASTER EXPLAINED THAT DESPITE HOWEVER MANY YEARS THEY HAD BEEN PRACTICING AT THE CENTER, THEY WERE STILL LIVING ACCORDING TO THEIR BODY SYSTEM. THEY HAD ONLY A SHALLOW UNDERSTANDING OF THEIR STRUCTURE, CAUSING THEM TO REMAIN IN THEIR CURRENT SITUATION.

UNSATISFIED WITH THE ANSWER, CONNEE KEPT PRESSING THE ZEN MASTER TO EXPEDITE THE STUDENTS' PROGRESS AND HAVE THEM GO BEYOND. SHE POINTED OUT THAT THERE WERE MANY WITH GREAT POTENTIAL TO UNDERSTAND ALL THIS.

"THEY ALL HAVE GREAT POTENTIAL. HOWEVER, THEY ARE PRACTICING WITH THEIR BODY, NOT AS SPIRITUAL BEINGS. IT ONLY TAKES A SPLIT SECOND TO REALIZE AND BE FREE FROM IT. HOWEVER, THEY ARE TRAPPED IN A PROTECTIVE SHIELD CREATED BY THE BODY, THINKING THEY ARE VERY SAFE AND THAT THEY KNOW EVERYTHING.

LITTLE DO THEY KNOW THAT ONCE THEY GET OUT OF IT, THE WORLD SUDDENLY WIDENS BEFORE THEM AND THEY REALIZE THAT THEY'VE BEEN SEEING THE WORLD THROUGH A MERE PIN HOLE."

"WELL, SINCE YOU HAVE THE POWER, SO TO SPEAK, WHY NOT LIFT THEM UP? SO THEY CAN SEE AND MOVE TO THE NEXT LEVEL."

"I THOUGHT SO TOO AT FIRST. SO, I POURED ALL I COULD INTO THEM. THEY APPRECIATED THE LIFT I GAVE THEM, BUT INSTEAD OF USING IT FOR THEIR PRACTICE, THEY WASTED IT ON THEIR OLD HABITS."

"WHY DIDN'T YOU MAKE THEM UNDERSTAND WHAT HAD JUST HAPPENED AND SHOW THEM WHAT THEY WERE SUPPOSED TO DO?"

"YOU ARE OPERATING FROM A VERY LOGICAL MIND.

EVERY TIME I ELEVATED THEM, THEY'D GO RIGHT BACK IN DESPITE MY TELLING THEM NOT TO. IT'S BECAUSE THEY ARE IN THEIR EGO SYSTEM, AND THEIR EGO SYSTEM WON'T ALLOW THEM TO GO BEYOND THE BUBBLE AND WILL ALWAYS PULL THEM RIGHT BACK IN. THEY ARE ATTACHED TO THEIR EGO SYSTEM AND THEIR BODY STRUCTURE, AND HAVE NO AWARENESS.

ONLY WHEN THEY REALIZE WHAT IS ACTUALLY HAPPENING CAN THEY WALK OUT ON THEIR OWN AND ESCAPE THE BUBBLE."

CONNEE STILL INSISTED THAT THIS WASN'T FAIR AND THAT HE, AS ZEN MASTER SHOULD MAKE THEM SEE AND HAVE THEM GO WHERE THEY NEEDED TO GO.

THE ZEN MASTER AGAIN POINTED OUT THAT IT WASN'T HIS ROLE TO FORCE HIS STUDENTS TO BE AT ZEN MASTER LEVEL WHEN THEY WEREN'T EVEN READY. HE WAS THERE TO HELP THEM CULTIVATE THE SEED TO ENLIGHTENMENT. AND THIS WORK WAS PRECIOUS TO HIM. EVERYONE WAS RESPONSIBLE FOR MAKING THEIR OWN CHOICES, EVEN IF THOSE CHOICES TURNED OUT TO BE WRONG. IT WAS ALL A PROCESS OF REALIZING.

THE ZEN MASTER'S OWN TRAINING HAD TAKEN A LONG TIME, SO HE WANTED TO SPEED UP HIS STUDENTS' PROGRESS. HOWEVER, HE REALIZED THAT SOME OF THEM WERE GOING TO TAKE THEIR OWN SWEET TIME DESPITE HIS HELP.

I'M THINKING THAT I'M NOT IN THE EGO SYSTEM.

WHEN YOU SAY SOMETHING LIKE THAT, YOU ARE ALREADY IN IT, EVEN WITHOUT REALIZING IT.

THE MOMENT YOU BEGIN TO THINK, CLING, AND BELIEVE, YOU FALL RIGHT BACK INTO THE EGO SYSTEM.

YOU MUST SIMPLY "BE", WITHOUT THINKING, AND WITHOUT CONVINCING.

THAT MAY BE SO, EVEN AS I SPEAK. BUT I WANT TO FIND A WAY FOR THEM TO UNDERSTAND AND SOLVE THIS PROBLEM AND PULL THEM OUT OF THERE.

HOW DO YOU PLAN TO DO THAT?

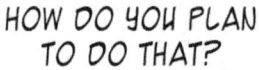

I DON'T KNOW, BUT THERE MUST BE A WAY. OTHERWISE, THERE'S A LOT OF USELESS AND WORTHLESS SUFFERING IN THIS WORLD.

WELL, THEN DO SOMETHING.

I DON'T HAVE THE WISDOM TO SAVE OTHERS. I NEED TO SAVE ME FIRST.

BEING CONNECTED

CONNEE FOUND HERSELF HAPPIER AND MORE CONTENT AS THE DAYS PASSED. IT SHOWED IN HER ATTITUDE TOWARDS HERSELF AND OTHERS, ENOUGH SO THAT THE ZEN MASTER TOOK NOTICE. HE ASKED CONNEE WHAT WAS CAUSING THIS CHANGE IN HER.

"IF THIS IS A DREAM STATE, I DON'T WANT TO WAKE UP FROM IT. AND I DON'T EVEN KNOW IF I CAN EXPLAIN IT PROPERLY."

"TRY IT ANYWAY."

"I'VE BEEN TRYING TO MAKE AN INNER CONNECTION - SORT OF LIKE TRYING TO MAKE A PHONE CALL. I WOULD KEEP CALLING, BUT EITHER THE LINE WAS TOO BUSY, OR THERE WAS NO CONNECTION AT ALL. SOMETIMES, I WOULD PUT IT ON AUTO DIAL AND LISTEN FOR A CONNECTION WHILE I DID MY DAILY ROUTINE."

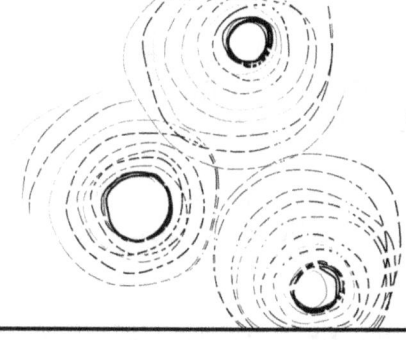

"ONE DAY, I FELT THE DIFFERENT PARTS OF MY BODY RESPONDING TO EACH OTHER AND CONNECTING. THIS FELT LIKE IT WAS HAPPENING AT THE CELLULAR LEVEL. I KEPT WATCH AS I EXPERIENCED THIS CHANGE, AND ONE DAY, IT ALL CAME TOGETHER AS ONE. I COULDN'T BELIEVE THAT MY CALL HAD FINALLY GONE THROUGH!"

"FROM EITHER SIDE OF THE LINE, THERE WAS ONLY SILENCE BECAUSE NOTHING NEEDED TO BE SAID. THE CONNECTION WAS ENOUGH. ALL MY MENTAL CHATTER AND EMOTIONAL DISHARMONY STOPPED. IN ITS PLACE WAS A SENSE OF PROFOUND PEACE AND SERENITY. I HAD MADE THE WHOLE BODY AND MIND CONNECTION. HOW WAS THIS POSSIBLE?"

"I'VE HAD THIS FOR A FEW WEEKS NOW, AND I WANT IT TO CONTINUE."

"INTERESTING! THOUGH NO ONE HAS QUITE EXPLAINED IT THE WAY YOU JUST DID, THAT'S THE GENERAL DESCRIPTION OF SUCH AN EVENT."

THE ZEN MASTER EXPLAINED THAT HER INDIVIDUAL ORGANS THAT HAD BEEN WORKING INDEPENDENTLY FROM ONE ANOTHER HAD FINALLY COME TOGETHER TO CREATE A HARMONIOUS WHOLE. THIS ALLOWED THE THE MISSING LINK TO ARRIVE FINALLY.

WHEN THE SIX ORGANS DIDN'T FUNCTION IN HARMONY, THE MIND WAS ALSO AFFECTED. THIS CREATED DISCORDANT THOUGHTS THAT DIDN'T HAVE THE ABILITY TO VIEW THE WORLD CLEARLY. MANY OF US WERE IN THIS STATE.

OUR BODY SYSTEM NATURALLY DESIRED TO FUNCTION HARMONIOUSLY, EVEN THOUGH OUR DYSFUNCTIONAL MIND FAILED TO RECOGNIZE IT AS SUCH. SO WHEN SOMEONE HAD A STRONG DESIRE TO RETURN TO THEIR PLACE OF ORIGIN, THAT PERSON WAS ACTUALLY SEEKING THE TOTAL UNIFICATION OF THE MIND AND BODY—THE ORIGINAL PERFECT STATE.

UNFORTUNATELY, THE ENTRENCHED DYSFUNCTION IN THE SYSTEM RESISTED SUCH CHANGE, AND THE MIND OFTEN CAME UP WITH COUNTLESS REASONS TO DO NOTHING AND REMAIN DYSFUNCTIONAL.

THE ONLY WAY TO BREAK THROUGH THIS DISFUNCTION WAS TO ALIGN AND HARMONIZE THE SIX ORGANS. THIS JOB BELONGED TO THAT PERSON'S "TRUE NATURE", THE INNER GUIDE.

IN CONNEE'S CASE, HER SIX ORGANS WERE ALIGNED AND HARMONIZED, THANKS TO THE HERBS, SUN DOH, SUN DOH DIET REGIME, AND ZEN PRACTICE. IF SHE WANTED TO PRESERVE THIS HARMONIOUS CONNECTION, IT WAS CRUCIAL THAT SHE MAINTAINED THE SIX-ORGAN SYSTEM WELL—ALONG WITH ZEN MIND. IT WAS ALSO THE KEY TO HAVING QUALITY LONGEVITY.

EVEN A BRIEF NEGLECT OF THIS SYSTEM COULD CAUSE CONNEE TO BECOME COCKY AND QUICKLY SHATTER THE DELICATE BALANCE OF HER MIND AND BODY CONNECTION.

"THEN I DON'T UNDERSTAND HOW YOU CAN EVEN ACHIEVE THIS IF YOU ARE ISOLATED IN THE MOUNTAINS, WITHOUT RESOURCES. HOW DID YOU AND OTHERS IN THE MONASTERY DO IT?"

"IT WASN'T EASY. UNLIKE HERE WHERE EVERYTHING IS PROVIDED, WE NEVER HAD ENOUGH FOOD IN THE MONASTERY BACK THEN."

ONE DAY, I FOLLOWED ONE OF THE ZEN MASTERS ON HIS DAILY WALK IN THE MOUNTAINS. I COULDN'T UNDERSTAND HOW HE COULD SO ACTIVELY SERVE HIS STUDENTS AND LAITY WHILE EATING SO LITTLE FOOD AT THE TEMPLE. I SAW HIM EAT ONLY TWO TO THREE LEAVES ON HIS WALK. THAT WAS ENOUGH TO SUPPLY WHAT HIS BODY NEEDED. HE LATER TOLD ME THAT EATING RAW FOODS DELIVERED 90 TO 100 PERCENT OF THEIR NUTRIENTS INTO OUR SYSTEM WHILE COOKED FOODS ONLY PROVIDED 20-30% AND WASTED THE REST.

"CURRENTLY, YOUR BODY IS PURIFYING AND HARMONIZING AT THE SAME TIME, ALLOWING YOU TO FOCUS ON YOUR PRACTICE. WHAT YOU EAT IS TAILORED TO YOUR UNIQUE BODY STRUCTURE. THIS METHOD REQUIRES THE DIET TO BE TAILORED DIFFERENTLY FROM PERSON TO PERSON. THOUGH THERE MAY BE SIMILARITIES BETWEEN PEOPLE, THEY WILL NEVER BE AN EXACT MATCH."

THE ZEN MASTER THEN WARNED CONNEE NOT TO BECOME ENAMORED WITH THIS TRANSFORMATION AS IT HINDERED HER PROGRESS. MOST PEOPLE GOT EXCITED OVER THIS EVENT AND WERE TEMPTED TO JUST LINGER FOREVER IN THIS STATE, HALTING THEIR GROWTH.

"I SEE. THEN I WILL LET IT ALL GO, AND KEEP ONLY THE AWARENESS."

TWENTY-ONE DAYS TO HONOR HER PARENTS

ONE DAY, CONNEE TOLD THE ZEN MASTER THAT SHE WISHED TO TAKE TWENTY-ONE DAYS TO GO VISIT HER PARENTS. HER PRACTICE HAD MADE HER REALIZE THAT SHE HAD NEVER PROPERLY THANKED HER PARENTS. SHE WISHED TO TRULY GET TO KNOW WHO THEY WERE AS INDIVIDUALS AND WHAT THEIR WISHES WERE. CONNEE INTENDED TO LISTEN AND HONOR ALL THEIR WISHES DURING THE TWENTY-ONE DAYS THERE.

WHEN THE ZEN MASTER POINTED OUT THAT HONORING ALL THE WISHES OF HER PARENTS WOULD BE MET WITH DIFFICULTIES, CONNEE ASSURED HIM THAT THEY WERE REASONABLE PEOPLE. THEY WOULD NOT MAKE ANY UNREASONABLE REQUESTS, AND EVEN IF THEY DID, SHE INTENDED TO FULFILL THEM TO THE EXTENT OF HER ABILITIES.

"YOU WILL BE ABLE TO DO THAT WITHOUT YOUR STRONG OPINIONS?"

"I KNOW NOW THAT I DON'T HAVE TO HONOR MY OPINIONS. THEY'RE JUST OPINIONS AFTERALL. NO POINT IN FOLLOWING WHAT DOES NOT COME FROM THE INSIDE."

CONNEE RECEIVED PERMISSION FROM THE ZEN MASTER AND LEFT FOR HER PARENTS' HOME. WHEN SHE ARRIVED, SHE WAS GREETED WARMLY BY HER MOTHER AND FATHER. CONNEE COULD TELL THAT THEY HADN'T RECEIVED VISITORS FOR A LONG TIME.

FROM DAY ONE, CONNEE CLEANED HOUSE, DID LAUNDRY, SHOPPED AND COOKED EVERY MEAL FOR THEM. THE MEALS SHE SERVED WERE TAILORED TO HER PARENTS' PREFERENCE, NOT CONNEE'S. HER PARENTS COULDN'T BELIEVE THE CHANGE IN CONNEE'S BEHAVIOR AND ATTITUDE. SHE HAD BEEN THE YOUNGEST IN THE FAMILY, SO SHE WAS NEVER EXPECTED TO DO ANY OF THE HOUSE CHORES.

WHEN THE FATHER GENTLY ADMONISHED HER FOR DOING TOO MUCH WORK AND TOLD HER NOT TO OVERDO IT, CONNEE SUGGESTED THAT THEY PLAY CARDS. WHEN HER FATHER SUGGESTED THAT THEY PLAY FOR PENNIES, CONNEE TOLD HIM THAT THERE WOULD BE NO GIVING BACK THE WINNINGS. EVERYONE HAPPILY AGREED.

CONNEE HAD BEEN LOOKING FOR AN OPPORTUNITY TO BRING THIS UP. SHE KNEW THAT HER MOTHER'S GENERAL HEALTH HADN'T BEEN GOOD FOR A WHILE. WITH DARK EXPRESSION, HER FATHER EXPLAINED THAT THE DOCTOR HAD TOLD HER BROTHER THAT MOTHER'S FEMALE ORGANS WERE INFECTED WITH CANCER CELLS. THERE WAS NO CURE, AND SHE WOULD BE LIVING LIKE THIS FOR THE REMAINDER OF HER LIFE. THIS WAS WHY SHE COULD NOT WALK.

EVERYONE SAT IN SILENCE FOR SOME TIME. THEN LOOKING AT HER PARENTS, CONNEE ASKED THEM IF SHE HAD EVER HURT ANYONE, WHETHER INTENTIONALLY OR UNINTENTIONALLY. AND SHE ASKED IF SHE WAS EVER A PROBLEM CHILD.

CONNEE'S MOTHER EAGERLY SHARED HER MEMORIES OF CONNEE, THE YOUNGEST OF HER TEN CHILDREN. TWO OF HER CHILDREN HAD DIED EARLIER FROM COMMON CHILDHOOD DISEASES SINCE VACCINES WEREN'T AVAILABLE BACK THEN. AS THE YOUNGEST, CONNEE WAS NEVER DEMANDING LIKE HER SIBLINGS HAD BEEN. SHE WOULD SIT QUIETLY, GAZING AT THE HORIZON.

"I COULDN'T REACH YOU LIKE THE OTHER KIDS. WHEN THE ADULTS DIDN'T DISMISS YOU LIKE A CHILD, I THOUGHT IT WAS OUT OF THEIR RESPECT FOR YOUR FATHER. BUT NO, THAT WASN'T IT. IT WAS ALL YOU."

"YOU WERE VERY INDEPENDENT. IT IS VERY TOUGH FOR A MOTHER WHEN THE CHILD DOESN'T NEED ANYTHING FROM HER. IT WAS A VERY UNCOMFORTABLE AND LONELY FEELING TO HAVE AS A MOTHER. BUT YOU WERE NEVER A PROBLEM CHILD."

"I AM SORRY, MOM. SOMETIMES I WONDERED ABOUT THAT."

THEN CONNEE ASKED HER FATHER ABOUT HIS MEMORIES OF HER.

SMILING WARMLY, HE TOLD HER THAT SHE WAS DIFFERENT FROM ALL HER SIBLINGS. AS A CHILD, CONNEE HAD BEEN CONTENT TO BE BY HERSELF, WAS STRONG, INDEPENDENT, BOTH FAIR AND OPINIONATED. SHE TOOK CARE OF THE WEAKER KIDS AND WENT AFTER BULLIES.

HER FATHER REMEMBERED CONNEE TEACHING THE KIDS WHAT WAS RIGHT AND WRONG. AND SHE HAD NOT STOPPED THERE. IF THE ADULTS HAD MADE A MISTAKE, SHE WOULD POINT THAT OUT TOO. THEY DIDN'T LIKE THAT, BUT THEY AGREED WITH WHAT SHE SAID.

CONNEE COULD GET AWAY WITH THIS BECAUSE SHE SAID EVERYTHING IN A MATTER-OF-FACT WAY, WITHOUT EMOTION ATTACHED. SHE MERELY POINTED OUT WHAT SHE THOUGHT WAS WRONG, AND AS AN ADULT, THEY COULDN'T ARGUE BACK.

THOUGH IT WAS INTERESTING TO WATCH THE ADULTS TREAD CAREFULLY AROUND CONNEE, HER FATHER TOLD HER THAT SHE HAD NEVER BEEN MALICIOUS OR HAD INTENTIONALLY HURT SOMEONE.

CONNEE WAS RELIEVED TO HEAR IT.

THEN CONNEE LOOKED AT HER MOTHER.

"MOM, CAN YOU TRUST ME WITH YOUR LIFE?"

"OF COURSE I TRUST YOU WITH MY LIFE."

"I MAY BE ABLE TO TREAT YOUR CONDITION. HOWEVER, IT IS VERY RISKY. WITH ONE MISTAKE, YOU CAN DIE FROM IT. DOCTORS WILL THINK IT'S CRAZY TO EVEN TRY IT."

"CAN YOU TRUST ME ENOUGH TO TRY IT?"

CONNEE'S FATHER WONDERED HOW SHE COULD HELP HER MOTHER. CONNEE EXPLAINED THAT SHE KNEW ABOUT HERBS. SHE NEEDED TO COOL DOWN HER MOTHER'S BODY SYSTEM, BUT FOR IT TO WORK, SHE WOULD NEED TO BRING THE BODY TEMPERATURE DOWN TO VERY DANGEROUS LEVELS. IT WOULD BE ONLY AFTER THAT SHE COULD TREAT THE ACTUAL CONDITION.

WHEN SHE EXPLAINED THE CONTENTS OF THE HERB FORMULA SHE WAS PLANNING TO USE, HER FATHER CONFIRMED THAT HER MOTHER HAD TAKEN THOSE IN THE PAST WITHOUT PROBLEMS.

"IF I CAN GET ANY RELIEF, I WILL TAKE THE CHANCE. IT'S TERRIBLE LIVING IN THIS CONDITION. I OFTEN WONDER WHAT I'VE DONE TO DESERVE THIS."

"MOM, IT'S NOT ANYTHING YOU DID. IT'S JUST YOUR BODY STRUCTURE."

"MOM, THIS IS A DELICATE PROCEDURE SO I NEED YOU TO FOLLOW MY INSTRUCTIONS PRECISELY. CAN YOU DO THAT?"

CONNEE'S MOTHER ASSURED HER THAT SHE WOULD FOLLOW HER DIRECTIONS PRECISELY. WHEN HER FATHER ASKED CONNEE WHERE SHE HAD LEARNED ALL THIS, SHE REPLIED THAT SHE HAD GAINED ALL THIS KNOWLEDGE FROM HER OWN ILLNESS AND FROM HER TEACHER IN SAN FRANCISCO.

THE FOLLOWING DAY, CONNEE WENT TO GATHER THE NECESSARY HERBS. AFTER BEING REFUSED BY THREE DIFFERENT HERBALISTS WHO RECOGNIZED THE FORMULA AS DANGEROUS, CONNEE WAS FORCED TO GET THE HERBS SEPARATELY FROM DIFFERENT VENDORS. BACK AT HOME, CONNEE CAREFULLY MEASURED OUT THE HERBS AND BREWED THEM.

AS CONNEE WAS PREPARING THE HERBS, HER BROTHER STOPPED BY. TAKING HER ASIDE, HE TOLD HER THAT EVEN THE BEST DOCTORS HAD GIVEN UP ON THEIR MOTHER'S CONDITION. HE DIDN'T WANT CONNEE TO GIVE THEM FALSE HOPE. CONNEE KNEW THAT HER BROTHER HAD NEVER DELIVERED THE HERBS SHE HAD SENT FROM SAN FRANCISCO TO EASE HER MOTHER'S PAINS. HOWEVER, SHE DIDN'T MENTION THAT. SHE SIMPLY TOLD HIM NOT TO WORRY, THAT SHE WAS PLAYING THE ROLE OF CARING DAUGHTER WHILE SHE WAS THERE.

WHEN CONNEE'S MOTHER TOOK THE FIRST SERVING OF THE MEDICINE, NOTHING HAPPENED. WITH THE SECOND SERVING, SHE FELT CALMER AND COULD FEEL THE COOLING SYSTEM WORKING. THE THIRD SERVING COOLED HER FACE AND EXTREMITIES WHILE THE FOURTH CAUSED HER BODY TO SHIVER. BECAUSE HER BODY HAD TO BE THOROUGHLY CHILLED FOR THE NEXT FORMULA TO WORK, THE MOTHER TOOK THE FIFTH AND SIXTH SERVINGS WHICH BROUGHT HER TO A PRE-FROZEN STATE.

WITH THE SEVENTH SERVING BEING THE SECOND FORMULA, THE MOTHER'S BODY STABILIZED AND FELL INTO A RELAXED MODE, ALLOWING HER TO SLEEP DEEPLY AND RESTFULLY. CONNEE'S MOTHER NOTICEABLY IMPROVED WITH EACH SERVING, AND BY THE TIME SHE TOOK THE FOURTEENTH SERVING SHE WAS ABLE TO WALK.

ONE DAY, CONNEE HEARD HER MOTHER SCREAMING FOR HER TO COME. WORRIED, CONNEE HURRIED TO HER ROOM AND FOUND HER MOTHER REACHING OUT TO CONNEE WITH TEARS RUNNING DOWN HER FACE. THE FATHER ALSO RUSHED IN, HAVING HEARD THE SCREAM.

HOLDING ON TO CONNEE'S HANDS, THE MOTHER EXPLAINED THAT HER PROLAPSED UTERUS HAD GONE BACK IN. CONNEE WAS SURPRISED AND GRATEFUL.

"I DON'T KNOW HOW TO THANK YOU! IT'S GOTTEN SO MUCH BETTER."

"YOU DID ALL THE WORK AND MADE THIS POSSIBLE. ONLY YOU CAN SAVE YOU. I'M SO PROUD OF YOU, MOM!"

ALL THREE OF THEM STOOD WITH JOYFUL TEARS IN THEIR EYES, GRATEFUL THAT MOTHER COULD NOW HAVE A BETTER QUALITY OF LIFE.

A FEW DAYS LATER HER FATHER ASKED HER IF SHE COULD HELP OTHERS WHO WERE SUFFERING A GREAT DEAL. CONNEE HAD TO EXPLAIN THAT SHE WAS NOT A PROFESSIONAL DOCTOR NOR AN HERBALIST. SHE HAD TAKEN A BIG GAMBLE ON HER MOTHER'S LIFE BECAUSE SHE COULDN'T BEAR TO WATCH HER SUFFER EVERY DAY.

WHEN HER FATHER INSISTED THAT HE HAD WITNESSED HER ABILITY WITH THE MOTHER'S TREATMENT, CONNEE REMINDED HIM THAT IT WAS PURE LUCK ON HER PART AND THE HELPING HANDS FROM ABOVE. CONNEE INSISTED THIS WAS A MIRACLE BROUGHT ON BY MOTHER'S FAITH, AND SHE HAD ONLY ASSISTED.

CONNEE MADE HER PARENTS PROMISE THAT THEY WOULD KEEP THESE EVENTS TO THEMSELVES. SHE HAD TO CONTINUE ON HER JOURNEY AND COULD NOT BE SIDETRACKED INTO HERBS, EVEN THOUGH IT WAS AN IMPORTANT TOOL FOR HER JOURNEY.

WHAT ABOUT FAMILY MEMBERS?

ONLY THREE OF US MUST KNOW. DO I HAVE YOUR WORD?

YES, I UNDERSTAND. I'VE KEPT QUIET ALL MY LIFE, SO THAT'S EASY.

CONNEE THANKED HER PARENTS FOR TRUSTING HER AND KEEPING THIS TO THEMSELVES. SHE ALSO PREPARED HERBS FOR HER FATHER AND SHARED WHAT SHE HAD LEARNED FROM THE ZEN MASTER. HER FATHER ENJOYED ADDING THIS KNOWLEDGE TO HIS CACHE OF INFORMATION HE HAD COLLECTED OVER THE YEARS.

FATHER'S LIFE-LONG DREAM

ONE EVENING, CONNEE'S FATHER SHARED A LIFE-LONG DREAM THAT HE HAD SO FAR FAILED TO REALIZE. HE HAD TRIED FOR DECADES TO ACCOMPLISH THIS BEFORE HIS EARTHLY DEPARTURE. HIS SONS HAD PROMISED HIM THAT WHEN THEY BECAME WEALTHY ENOUGH, THEY WOULD HELP. NOW, IN ALL THEIR WEALTH, THE SONS WERE DISMISSING HIS DREAMS AS IMPRACTICAL AND SENILE.

THE FATHER HAD TURNED TO THE DAUGHTERS WHO HAD ALSO ACCUMULATED CONSIDERABLE WEALTH, BUT NOTHING CAME OF IT. NO ONE WANTED TO TALK ABOUT IT ANYMORE AND IT WAS CAUSING TREMENDOUS STRESS AMONG THE SONS AND DAUGHTERS.

CONNEE'S FATHER WAS NOW 88 YEARS OF AGE AND FELT HE WOULDN'T BE ABLE TO CLOSE HIS EYES IN DEATH IF HE FAILED TO FULFILL THIS DREAM. THIS HAD NEVER BEFORE BEEN SHARED WITH CONNEE BECAUSE SHE WAS THE BABY OF THE FAMILY AND THE SIBLINGS CONSIDERED THE IDEA CRAZY.

CONNEE FOR HER PART, KNEW THAT THIS DREAM WAS NEVER GOING TO HAPPEN. SHE KEPT THIS TO HERSELF. WHEN SHE ASKED HER FATHER WHY THIS DREAM WAS SO IMPORTANT TO HIM, HE TOLD HER THAT THIS WAS FOR THE FUTURE OF THE FAMILY.

"BUILDING A MONUMENTAL BUILDING AND A HOUSE FOR 100 PLUS FAMILY MEMBERS IS NOT AN EASY TASK. PEOPLE CAN'T UNDERSTAND THIS CONCEPT TO BEGIN WITH. IT MUST MAKE PRACTICAL SENSE, BOTH LOGICALLY AND FINANCIALLY."

"FOR THE SAKE OF OUR ENTIRE FAMILY, WE MUST. ONCE WE BUILD IT, THINGS WILL BEGIN TO CHANGE, CALM DOWN, AND THINGS WILL MOVE OUT OF CHAOS. RIGHT NOW, WE ARE IN CHAOS AS A FAMILY AND AS INDIVIDUALS. THAT WILL ALL CHANGE ONCE WE ERECT THE BUILDING."

"HOW WILL ANYONE EVEN BEGIN THIS HUGE PROJECT WITHOUT UNDERSTANDING IT? THAT'S THE DILEMMA."

"NO LOGICAL MIND WOULD UNDERSTAND. THE UNDERSTANDING WILL COME LATER."

AT THE TIME, CONNEE DIDN'T HAVE THE CAPACITY TO COMPREHEND HER FATHER'S REASONING. HOWEVER, SHE LISTENED QUIETLY TO HER FATHER OVER MANY DAYS WITHOUT EXPRESSING HER OWN OPINIONS. SHE COULD TELL THAT HE WASN'T THINKING FROM HIS EGO AND WAS CONCERNED FOR THE FAMILY'S FUTURE.

AT THE END OF THE STAY, CONNEE PROMISED HER FATHER THAT IF NO ONE HONORED HIS WISH UPON HIS DEATH, SHE WOULD SEE WHAT COULD BE DONE FOR THE FAMILY. HER FATHER THANKED HER AND SAID HE WOULD CONTINUE TRYING TO CONVINCE HIS SONS TO HONOR THEIR RESPONSIBILITY TILL HIS DYING BREATH.

LEAVING SAN FRANCISCO - A NECESSARY DEPARTURE

SOME TIME AFTER SHE RETURNED TO SAN FRANCISCO, CONNEE KNEW IT WAS TIME TO LEAVE. HOWEVER, WHEN SHE THOUGHT ABOUT ALL THE THINGS THAT THE ZEN MASTER HAD PROVIDED FOR HER, SHE JUST COULDN'T DO IT. NOT ONLY DID THE ZEN MASTER MAKE HER A HEALTHY BODY, HE ALSO GAVE HER MENTAL AND SPIRITUAL WELLBEING. SHE OWED HIM A GREAT DEBT OF GRATITUDE.

THIS CONFLICT WAS EATING HER UP. SOMETHING DEEP WITHIN HER KNEW SHE HAD TO LEAVE, BUT IT DIDN'T SEEM A GOOD ENOUGH REASON TO GIVE THE ZEN MASTER. WAS IT SUFFICIENT TO EXPLAIN THAT SHE HAD TO BE SOMEWHERE ELSE, THOUGH SHE DIDN'T KNOW WHERE THAT WAS?

WAS IT RIGHT TO SAY THIS TO SOMEONE WHO HAD SAVED HER, HELPED AND STRENGTHENED HER, AND HAD SHOWN HER WHO SHE WAS? HOW COULD SHE ABANDON HIM LIKE THIS? SURELY, STAYING AND HELPING HIM WAS THE RIGHT THING TO DO.

UNABLE TO SAY ANYTHING TO THE ZEN MASTER AS SHE AGONIZED OVER THIS, CONNEE DECIDED TO CALL JACK. SHE EXPLAINED HER DILEMMA OVER THE PHONE, AND JACK REPLIED IN HIS USUAL STRAIGHT FORWARD MANNER.

HE REMINDED CONNEE THAT THE ZEN CENTER WAS NOT HER TRUE DESTINATION, AND THAT SHE HAD TO MOVE ON.

CONNEE AGREED WITH JACK. BUT WHEN SHE LOOKED AROUND THE ZEN CENTER AND HER BELOVED TEACHER, SHE COULD NOT SPEAK UP. SHE STAYED AND CONTINUED TO ENDURE THE AGONIZING CALLING FROM WITHIN.

"I'M SORRY ... I KNOW THAT SOME PART OF ME IS STILL SICK, WHILE ANOTHER PART ISN'T."

"THIS ONE DECISION DEFINITELY DOES NOT COME FROM THE SICK MIND. I KNOW."

WHEN THE ZEN MASTER DEMANDED HOW SHE KNEW THE DIFFERENCE, CONNEE TOLD HIM THAT SHE HAD CHECKED HER MOTIVES FOR MONTHS AND FOUND NOTHING TO LINK IT TO OTHER THAN THAT SHE HAD TO BE SOMEWHERE ELSE. THERE WAS NO INFORMATION ON WHERE TO GO OR WHOM TO MEET. IT WAS INSANE, BUT SHE HAD TO FOLLOW HER INNER GUIDANCE.

THE ZEN MASTER WAS VISIBLY UPSET AND HAD TO CALM HIMSELF DOWN A BIT BEFORE ASKING CONNEE WHEN SHE WAS PLANNING TO LEAVE.

"AS SOON AS POSSIBLE."

"AND YOU'RE TELLING ME THIS NOW?"

"I AGONIZED OVER THIS FOR MONTHS, CONVINCING MYSELF NOT TO GO. FROM THE START, I TOLD YOU THAT I WAS ALREADY LATE."

"I THOUGHT IT WAS YOUR SICK MIND SPEAKING."

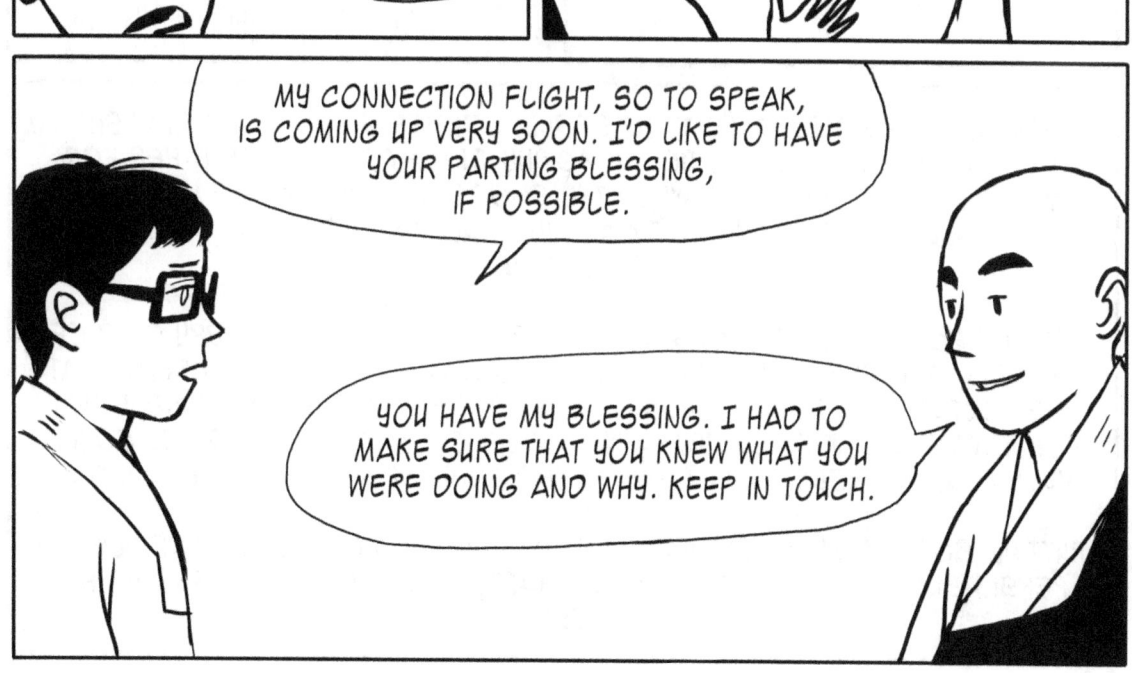

"MY CONNECTION FLIGHT, SO TO SPEAK, IS COMING UP VERY SOON. I'D LIKE TO HAVE YOUR PARTING BLESSING, IF POSSIBLE."

"YOU HAVE MY BLESSING. I HAD TO MAKE SURE THAT YOU KNEW WHAT YOU WERE DOING AND WHY. KEEP IN TOUCH."

FOLLOWING HER INNER GUIDANCE, CONNEE BOUGHT A PLANE TICKET TO SEOUL. AND ON THE DAY OF HER DEPARTURE, SHE BADE EVERYONE AT THE ZEN CENTER FAREWELL, SAVING HER LAST GOODBYE FOR THE ZEN MASTER.

SOLEMNLY, CONNEE BOWED THREE TIMES, EXPRESSING HER DEEP RESPECT AND GRATITUDE FOR HER BELOVED TEACHER.

HIGH UP IN THE AIR, HALFWAY TO SEOUL, CONNEE DISCOVERED THAT SHE NO LONGER FELT THE EMOTIONAL AGONY THAT HAD TORMENTED HER FOR MONTHS. THE CONFLICT BETWEEN THE EMOTIONAL URGENCY OF HER INNER GUIDE AND THE OPPOSING LOGICAL MIND HAD CAUSED GREAT CONFUSION IN CONNEE.

HER LOGICAL MIND HAD FOUGHT THE INNER GUIDE'S URGING EVERY STEP OF THE WAY, AND SHE COULD HAVE EASILY CONVINCED HERSELF TO REMAIN AT THE CENTER. EVENTUALLY, SHE WOULD HAVE REALIZED HER MISTAKE IN NOT FOLLOWING HER INNER GUIDE, HAVING BENEFITTED NO ONE. AND SHE COULD HAVE FOUND HERSELF SICK AGAIN, WITHOUT KNOWING WHAT HAD CAUSED IT.

PUTTING BOTH PALMS TOGETHER, CONNEE THANKED HER INNER GUIDE FOR ITS PERSISTENCE AND THANKED THE ZEN MASTER FOR HIS TEACHINGS AND HIS BLESSING.

PART III

RECLAIMED

MEETING MOTHER ZEN MASTER

UPON HER ARRIVAL IN SEOUL, CONNEE BEGAN SEARCHING FOR A DESTINATION.

ONE DAY SHE FOUND HERSELF AT A TEMPLE, WHICH WAS NOT ON HER LIST. SHE SPENT THE DAY DOING SITTING AND WALKING MEDITATIONS. GOING BACK TO THE MOTEL ONLY TO SLEEP, CONNEE SPENT HER DAYS AT THE TEMPLE FROM MORNING TO DUSK. SOMETHING WAS PULLING HER TO THE TEMPLE AND HOLDING HER THERE, BUT SHE DIDN'T KNOW WHAT.

AFTER SEVERAL DAYS, A YOUNG WOMAN APPROACHED CONNEE AND ASKED HER IF SHE WANTED TO MEET WITH MOTHER ZEN MASTER.

"OH, NO—I JUST LOVE BEING HERE. AM I BOTHERING ANYONE?"

"NO, NOT AT ALL. JUST SEEING IF YOU WANTED TO MEET WITH MOTHER ZEN MASTER. MANY PEOPLE WANT TO MEET HER, BUT SOMETIMES THEY HESITATE AND PONDER A BIT. WE PROVIDE MEALS HERE, SO WHY DON'T YOU LATER JOIN US?"

"OH YES, THE FOOD IS WONDERFUL HERE. THANK YOU."

"I AM SORRY I INTERRUPTED. PLEASE ENJOY THE WALK."

CONNEE CONTINUED TO VISIT THE TEMPLE EVERY DAY, AND GOT INTO A ROUTINE DESPITE PLANS TO VISIT SOMEWHERE ELSE. HER FEET KEPT DELIVERING HER TO THIS TEMPLE. SHE COULD NOT FIGURE OUT WHY, BUT SHE WAS STUCK HERE.

ONE DAY, A VOICE INTERRUPTED HER WALKING MEDITATION.

"YOU ARE HERE, BUT YOU DON'T KNOW WHY, HUH?"

THE MOTHER ZEN MASTER WELCOMED CONNEE. REMOVING EVERYONE FROM HER PRESENCE, SHE GAVE CONNEE HER FULL ATTENTION. THEY SHARED MANY LONG CONVERSATIONS.

HOWEVER, CONNEE STILL DID NOT KNOW WHY SHE WAS THERE.

WHAT HAD BROUGHT HER TO THIS PLACE AND TO MOTHER ZEN MASTER? THE CONNECTION SHE FELT WITH MOTHER ZEN MASTER WAS DEEP AND FAMILIAR, UNLIKE ANYTHING SHE HAD EXPERIENCED BEFORE.

YOU MUST KNOW... SO SNAP OUT OF IT!

LET ME KNOW THE REASON!

THE ZEN MASTER EXPLAINED TO CONNEE THAT EACH PERSON HAD A SPECIALTY IN THIS LIFE. SHE WAS NOT TO CONFINE HERSELF TO A GROUP OR PROJECTS. IF CONNEE CHOSE TO BELONG TO A GROUP, IT WOULD HINDER HER WORK. SHE WAS TO BE INDEPENDENT AND WORK FREELY.

THE ZEN MASTER TOLD HER TO BE FREE FROM ALL THOUGHTS AND CUSTOMS SO THAT SHE COULD WORK WITHOUT HINDRANCE AND BE TRULY FREE. SHE SHOULD NEVER COMPARE HERSELF TO OTHERS. THEY HAD THEIR OWN PATH COMPLETELY DIFFERENT FROM HERS.

CONNEE WAS TO WALK A UNIQUE PATH THAT WAS HERS ALONE TO DECODE. SHE WAS NEVER TO ACCEPT ANYONE'S DECODING OR THEIR UNDERSTANDING OF THE PATH SHE WAS TO TAKE. SHE WAS TO WHOLLY RELY ON HER *TRUE NATURE*. THE ZEN MASTER EMPHASIZED AGAIN THE IMPORTANCE OF THAT STATEMENT.

CONNEE DIDN'T FULLY UNDERSTAND WHAT THE ZEN MASTER MEANT BY IT. SHE SAID SHE WOULD REMEMBER THE ZEN MASTER'S WORDS AND EVENTUALLY UNDERSTAND IT BY WALKING THROUGH IT.

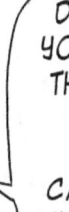

| THE ZEN WORLD - THE FIRST VISIT | MEETING WITH THE WHITE LION ZEN MASTER |

THEY WENT TO A DEEP SECLUDED ZEN RETREAT CENTER SET ALMOST NEAR THE TOP OF THE MOUNTAIN. NO ONE KNEW IT EXISTED EXCEPT FOR A HANDFUL OF ZEN MASTERS AND PRACTITIONERS.

THIS PLACE WAS OUT OF THE ORDINARY, LOCATED DEEP IN THE FOREST. NO HINT OF A BUILDING COULD BE SEEN FROM THE OUTSIDE. IT BLENDED COMPLETELY WITH THE FOREST.

THEY WERE WELL RECEIVED AND LATER, THE MASTER APPEARED, A BRIGHT WHITE LION OF POWERFUL AND COMMANDING PRESENCE.
THE LION ZEN MASTER WAS READY TO DEFEND HIS DHARMA WORLD. WHEN IT WAS TIME FOR DHARMA TALK BETWEEN THE ZEN MASTERS, CONNEE WAS ASKED TO LEAVE THE ROOM. SHE WAS NOT QUALIFIED TO BE PRESENT IN THAT CONVERSATION.

"SHE IS OKAY. SHE STAYS."

"YOU KNOW THE CUSTOM, AND YOU KNOW THE RULES. WE MUST HONOR OUR TRADITIONS."

THE HANDSOME WHITE LION WAS FEROCIOUS IN DEFENDING HIS DHARMA. THE DHARMA COMBATS BETWEEN TWO ZEN MASTERS WAS A WAY FOR THEM TO TEST THEIR ZEN KNOWLEDGE AND THEIR ZEN LEVELS. IT WAS UNACCEPTABLE TO HAVE A COMMONER WITNESS SUCH AN EVENT.

THE SECOND VISIT – MEETING WITH THE "S" MASTER

AGAIN, THEY WENT TO AN OFF-THE-GRID KIND OF PLACE. THIS TIME, IT WAS A GRAND OLD TEMPLE, SEVERAL HUNDRED YEARS OLD. A MONK GREETED THEM AND THE ZEN MASTER REQUESTED TO SEE THE MASTER OF THIS HUGE TEMPLE. THEY WERE GUIDED TO A LARGE GUEST ROOM.

CONNEE NOTICED THAT BESIDES BEING TREATED LIKE VIP GUESTS HERE, AND THE VAST SIZE OF THIS TEMPLE, IT WASN'T MUCH DIFFERENT FROM THE FIRST TEMPLE.

THOUGH THE FIRST TEMPLE HAD BEEN SMALLER AND A BIT HUMBLER, IT HAD BEEN ALIVE AND PRECISE. IT WAS LIKE ITS ZEN MASTER, THE WHITE LION, WITH FIERCE AND LIVING EYES THAT DID NOT MISS ANYTHING.

THE ZEN MASTER THAT LATER APPEARED TO GREET THEM LOOKED LIKE AN ORDINARY MONK WITH SOME POWER. HE CARRIED ON SMOOTHLY AND GRACEFULLY, ABSENT OF ROUGH EDGES.

TO CONNEE'S EYES, HIS WANTS AND DESIRES WERE ALL ATTACHMENTS. THIS ZEN MASTER WAS DIFFERENT FROM THE WHITE LION. EVEN THE WAY HER ZEN MASTER INTERACTED WITH THIS MASTER WAS DIFFERENT.

I WAS THINKING THAT IF ONE EXPERIENCED THE TRUE NATURE, ALL THINGS MELT AWAY. WHY ISN'T IT SO WITH THIS MASTER?

THE MEMORY OF HABITS REMAIN, LIKE A MOVIE YOU WATCHED LONG AGO. THE MOVIE CONTENT REMAINS IN YOUR MEMORY SYSTEM UNTIL SOMETHING TRIGGERS IT OR RELATES IT TO THE PRESENT. IT IS JUST HOW OUR SYSTEM WORKS. HOWEVER, ZEN IS ABOUT BEING AWARE OF AND LIVING IN THE PRESENT MOMENT. FOLLOWING THE MEMORY SYSTEM AS A POINT OF AWARENESS IS NOT ZEN. SOMETIMES, EVEN GREAT ZEN STUDENTS FORGET THAT AND BELIEVE THEY ARE AT PRESENT WITH THEIR MEMORY SYSTEM. THAT'S A DELUSIONAL STAGE.

DID HE CHOOSE TO BE HERE AS AN ABBOT TO THIS TEMPLE, OR WAS HE APPOINTED?

EVERYONE HAS A JOB TO DO — SOMETIMES BY CHOICE, AND SOMETIMES BY APPOINTMENT. THIS ABBOT IS GIVING HIS SERVICE TO THE TEMPLE, AND DOING HIS JOB WITH GREAT INTEGRITY.

THANK YOU.

THEIR DHARMA TALK WENT ON FOR HOURS.

THE TEMPLE ZEN MASTER OFFERED THEM LODGINGS AT THEIR TRADITIONAL FOLK VILLAGE. IT HAD BEEN MODERNIZED AND MAINTAINED BY THE TOWN'S PEOPLE AS A TOURIST ATTRACTION.

THEY HAPPILY ACCEPTED HIS OFFER AND FOUND THE OLD VILLAGE HOUSE COMFORTABLE.

NEXT MORNING, THE TEMPLE ZEN MASTER VISITED THEM AND INVITED THEM FOR A MEAL AT ONE OF THE VILLAGE RESTAURANTS. THE VILLAGE HAD QUITE A FEW SHOPS AND RESTAURANTS FOR TOURISTS.

THE TEMPLE MASTER TOLD CONNEE THAT THE VILLAGERS CALLED HIM THE "FENG SHUI MASTER". HE WAS PART OF THE COMMUNITY TO MAKE SURE THE VILLAGE WOULD SURVIVE FOR MANY YEARS. IN A WAY, THE VILLAGERS TREATED HIM AS A GUARDIAN OF THIS VILLAGE.

AFTER BREAKFAST, THE FENG SHUI MASTER GAVE THEM A TOUR OF THE TOWN AND EXPLAINED ITS HISTORY AND HOW IT HAD SURVIVED ALL THESE YEARS. THE GREAT ZEN MASTER WHO HAD CREATED THIS TOWN HAD APPLIED NATURE'S PHYSICS, ALSO KNOWN AS *FENG SHUI*, TO BRING HARMONY AND LONGEVITY.

CONNEE HAD NEVER HEARD OF FENG SHUI APPLIED THIS WAY AND ASKED HIM HOW IT COULD POSSIBLY WORK. THE FENG SHUI MASTER KINDLY TOOK CONNEE'S MANY QUESTIONS AND TRIED TO EXPLAIN IT AS EASILY AS POSSIBLE. HE SAID THAT NATURE AND OUR BODIES ARE THE SAME, WITH THE SAME PRINCIPLES APPLYING. THE PRINCIPLES, DEPENDING ON HOW THEY ARE APPLIED COULD CAUSE BOTH NATURE AND BODY TO EITHER PERISH OR FLOURISH IN HARMONIOUS EXISTENCE.

THE FENG SHUI MASTER INVITED CONNEE TO VISIT ANY TIME IF SHE HAD FURTHER QUESTIONS ON LIVING WITH NATURE HARMONIOUSLY. HE ALSO GAVE HER A BACK SCRATCHER MADE BY THE VILLAGERS.

YOU ARE VERY LUCKY AND VERY SPECIAL. I HOPE YOU KNOW THAT.

CONNEE DIDN'T UNDERSTAND WHAT HE MEANT BY IT. SHE THANKED HIM FOR HIS HOSPITALITY AND HIS TEACHING ON FENG SHUI.

THE FOURTH VISIT - ZEN MASTER'S OLD TEMPLE

THEIR NEXT STOP WAS WHERE CONNEE'S ZEN MASTER TRAINED AS A STUDENT. IT WAS AN ENORMOUS TEMPLE THAT HOUSED AN INTERNATIONAL ZEN CENTER. THE ZEN MASTER WAS WELL RECEIVED AND TREATED WITH GREAT RESPECT.

THEY WENT TO HAVE TEA WITH ONE OF THE HEAD ZEN TEACHERS AT THE INTERNATIONAL ZEN SCHOOL. AGAIN, CONNEE WAS ASKED TO LEAVE.

LET HER STAY. SHE SERVED AT THE SAN FRANCISCO ZEN CENTER FOR THE LAST TWO YEARS. I PROMISED HER THAT SHE WOULD GET A GLIMPSE OF THE ZEN WORLD. CAN YOU MAKE ONE EXCEPTION FOR HER?

YOU ARE VERY LUCKY. NO ONE IS ALLOWED TO COME INTO THIS ROOM UNLESS THEY ARE MASTERS, TEACHERS, AND STUDENTS OF THE ZEN WORLD. SO, YOU ARE VERY FORTUNATE TO HAVE A MASTER TO LET YOU IN THROUGH THE GATES. SHE HAS NEVER ASKED THIS OF ME, AND OUT OF RESPECT FOR HER, I WILL ALLOW IT.

THEY WENT ON WITH THE CONVERSATION FOR A FEW HOURS. THEY TALKED ABOUT THE ZEN STUDENTS, TREND OF ZEN PRACTITIONERS, AND WHO WAS IN LINE FOR THE TOP POSITION. THEY ALSO TALKED ABOUT FINANCIAL HARDSHIPS, THE CENTER'S BUILDING STRUCTURES, THE NECESSARY CHANGES, AND THEIR RETIREMENTS.

AFTERWARDS, THEY WENT TO THE TEMPLE'S DINING HALL. IT WAS LARGER THAN TWO FAST-FOOD RESTAURANTS PUT TOGETHER.

THE HALL WAS SPLIT INTO THREE DIFFERENT SEATING AREAS, ONE OF WHICH WAS RESERVED FOR HIGH-RANKING MONKS AND ZEN MASTERS. CONNEE'S ZEN MASTER GUIDED HER TO A TABLE, AND NOT KNOWING THE CULTURE NOR THE PROTOCOL, CONNEE SAT DOWN.

WHEN ONE OF THE MONKS CAME TO SERVE THEM, CONNEE'S ZEN MASTER TOLD THE MONK TO BRING CONNEE'S MEAL. THE MONK DIDN'T KNOW WHAT TO DO. SOMETHING WAS NOT RIGHT FOR HIM, AND HIS DISCOMFORT WAS OBVIOUS. HE HESITATED.

AT THAT MOMENT, CONNEE'S ZEN MASTER LEFT THE TABLE TO SPEAK WITH SOMEONE. THE MONK QUICKLY TOOK THIS OPPORTUNITY TO TELL CONNEE THAT SHE WAS SITTING IN THE WRONG AREA AND MUST GO. THIS AREA WAS RESERVED ONLY FOR HIGH RANKING MONKS, ZEN MASTERS, AND ABBOTS.

THE NEXT AREA WAS FOR NOVICE MONKS AND THERE WOULD BE NO ROOM FOR HER THERE EITHER. THE MONK TOLD HER THAT THIS PART OF THE BUILDING WAS NOT FOR COMMONERS AND LAITIES. SHE HAD TO GO TO ANOTHER PART OF THE BUILDING. THOUGH SHE DIDN'T KNOW WHERE THE MONK WAS DIRECTING HER, CONNEE TOLD HIM THAT SHE WOULD MOVE.

HOW COULD YOU NOT KNOW? YOU ARE LEARNING UNDER A GREAT ZEN MASTER. HOW COULD YOU NOT KNOW?

THIS IS MY FIRST TIME. PERHAPS MY MASTER IS TRYING TO TEACH ME THROUGH MY IGNORANCE. I AM SORRY.

YOU DON'T BELONG AT THIS TABLE.

THE EVENT

THE NEXT DAY AT THE TEMPLE, A HUGE CELEBRATION TOOK PLACE, HONORING THE PASSING AWAY OF A GREAT ZEN MASTER. CLOSE TO A THOUSAND ZEN MASTERS, TEACHERS, ABBOTS, VIPS, AND PRACTITIONERS ATTENDED. THE ZEN MASTERS SAT ACCORDING TO THEIR RANK, AND EVERYONE ELSE EITHER SAT OR STOOD BEHIND THEM. CONNEE, HOWEVER, WAS SEATED IN THE SECOND ROW OF THE FRONT SECTION, NEXT TO MOTHER ZEN MASTER.

AFTER THE EVENT, THE ZEN MASTER ASKED CONNEE WHAT SHE THOUGHT ABOUT THE PLACE.

SOMEHOW, IT FEELS LIKE I'VE BEEN HERE BEFORE.

BUT, I WOULDN'T STAY HERE, IF THAT IS WHAT YOU ARE ASKING.

OH, WHY IS THAT?

THAT'S NOT MY FUNCTION IN THIS LIFE.

AFTERWARDS, THE ZEN MASTER VISITED HER DHARMA SISTERS AND BROTHERS, AS WELL AS SEVERAL STUDENTS.

THE DEPARTURE

THIS TRIP HAD OPENED UP CONNEE'S WORLD. SHE REALIZED THAT HER ZEN MASTER WAS NOT AN ORDINARY ZEN MASTER. SHE WAS TRULY THE "MOTHER" AMONG ZEN MASTERS.

AS THEIR JOURNEY CONTINUED, CONNEE WAS LEFT SPEECHLESS AND IN AWE FROM THE PEOPLE AND PLACES THEY VISITED. SHE TRIED NOT TO ALLOW EMOTIONS OR LOGIC TO PLAY HAVOC ON THIS JOURNEY. AS MOTHER ZEN MASTER HAD ADVISED, SHE KEPT OBSERVING THROUGH THE UNMOVING MIND.

MOTHER ZEN MASTER SHOWED HER PLACES, PEOPLE AND EXPERIENCES SHE COULD NEVER HAVE HAD ACCESS TO ON HER OWN. IT WOULD HAVE TAKEN A LIFETIME ON HER OWN - IF SHE WAS LUCKY.

ONCE THE TRIP WAS OVER, THE MOTHER ZEN MASTER TOOK HER TO ONE OF CONNEE'S FAVORITE RESTAURANTS, TREATING HER TO A PLATEFUL OF FRESH VEGETABLES AS HER DEPARTING MEAL. WITHOUT OFFERING FURTHER GUIDANCE AS TO WHAT CONNEE SHOULD DO OR WHERE TO GO, OR AN INVITATION TO COME VISIT HER, THE MOTHER ZEN MASTER SIMPLY SENT HER OFF.

SHE WISHED CONNEE A GREAT JOURNEY TO HER DESTINATION. THIS FELT DISTANT, AND CONNEE WANTED SOMETHING WARMER TO CLING TO. WORDS LIKE: I WILL MISS YOU.

CONNEE BOWED THREE TIMES TO THE MOTHER ZEN MASTER FROM THE RESTAURANT FLOOR.

CONNEE WAS NOW ALONE WITH HER BACKPACK.
SHE HAD BEEN ALONE BEFORE, BUT THIS TIME IT HIT HER HARD FOR SHE STRANGELY FELT ALL ALONE IN THE UNIVERSE.

WITH TERRIBLE EMPTINESS SETTING IN, SHE WENT TO THE NEAREST PARK TO PROCESS ALL OF THE CHANGES. MANY PEOPLE CAME AND WENT AS SHE SAT ON THE METAL BENCH. SHE LET HER BODY MOURN AS A STEADY STREAM OF TEARS FLOWED DOWN HER FACE.

HOURS LATER, SHE GOT UP AND WENT TO A RESTAURANT BEFORE STARTING ON THE NEXT LEG OF HER JOURNEY HOME. PART OF HER STILL WANTED HER TEACHER'S PROTECTION, WORDS OF GUIDANCE, AND AN OFFER OF A PLACE TO RETURN TO.

WALKING LONG AND AIMLESSLY AFTER HER MEAL, CONNEE SUDDENLY HAD A REALIZATION.

"AH! SHE WANTS ME TO BE INDEPENDENT! TO BE WITHOUT PHYSICAL, MENTAL AND EMOTIONAL CRUTCHES. SHE WANTS ME TO BE FREE FROM ALL EXTERNAL MATTERS, AND TO BE ONE WITH MY **TRUE SELF**."

CONNEE STOPPED WALKING. ALL HER SHATTERED EMOTIONAL, MENTAL AND PHYSICAL STATES CAME BACK TOGETHER AS ONE, WITH GREAT CLARITY.

CONNEE TURNED AROUND AND GOT BACK ON HER PATH, CONFIDENT THAT SHE WOULD REACH HER DESTINATION AND GET BACK HOME.

MOUNT JIRI TRAINING CENTER

IN THE SPRING OF RED OX YEAR, CONNEE SOUGHT HER NEXT DESTINATION ON HER JOURNEY HOME.

SHE MET WITH PEOPLE AND VISITED PLACES IN SOUTH KOREA. SOME WERE GLAD TO ACCEPT HER, WHILE OTHERS FELT SHE DIDN'T MEET THEIR STANDARDS. AND SOME SIMPLY DIDN'T MEET CONNEE'S NEEDS.

WHILE THERE WERE MANY CHOICES BEFORE HER, CONNEE'S INNER DIRECTION TOLD HER THAT NONE OF THOSE WERE FOR HER.

EARLIER, CONNEE HAD MET A MAN WHO RECOMMENDED MOUNT JIRI TRAINING CENTER. AROUND THAT SAME TIME, ANOTHER PERSON HAD POINTED TO THE SAME PLACE AS WELL.

THE ORGANIZATION WAS HIGHLY REPUTABLE, KNOWN FOR ITS INTEGRITY. AND IT HAD CREATED THE MT. JIRI CENTER FOR SERIOUS PRACTITIONERS. CONNEE WAS ALREADY FAMILIAR WITH ITS PRACTICE THANKS TO THE SAN FRANCISCO ZEN MASTER'S TEACHINGS, AND SHE HAD BENEFITED GREATLY FROM IT.

CONNEE DECIDED TO CHECK OUT THE TRAINING CENTER. SHE DISCOVERED THAT ITS FACILITIES WERE BARE BONES WITH NO INDOOR PLUMBING. WITH THE NEAREST LODGING A COUPLE HOURS AWAY IN THE NEAREST CITY, SHE ACCEPTED AN OVERNIGHT STAY IN A SMALL ROOM SET APART FROM EVERYONE.

NEXT MORNING, SHE HAD TO WALK TO A SMALL STREAM TO WASH HERSELF. NOTHING BOTHERED HER. NOT EVEN THE OUTHOUSE. SHE FELT AN UNUSUALLY NURTURING PRESENCE THERE, AS IF SOMEONE OR SOMETHING WAS SUPPORTING HER.

FOLLOWING HER INNER GUIDANCE, CONNEE CHOSE THE MT. JIRI TRAINING CENTER AS HER NEXT DESTINATION. HERE, SHE FELT ENERGETICALLY NURTURED, WHICH WOULD ALLOW HER TO FOCUS SOLELY ON HER JOURNEY OF THE MIND.

THE MT. JIRI TRAINING CENTER WAS NOT A RELIGIOUS ORGANIZATION. THEIR TEACHING HAS EXISTED FOR ALMOST 10,000 YEARS, STAYING HIDDEN DEEP IN THE MOUNTAINS TO TRAIN ONLY SELECTED INDIVIDUALS. AND IT WAS ONLY IN RECENT SEVERAL DECADES THAT ONE OF THESE INDIVIDUALS HAD INTRODUCED THIS TEACHING TO THE MODERN WORLD FOR THE BENEFIT OF THE PEOPLE.

THERE WOULD BE NO WORSHIP OF ANYONE OR ANYTHING. HOWEVER, EVERYONE WAS REQUIRED TO FOLLOW THE TRAINING THEY PROVIDED, AND LIVE IN HARMONY WITH ALL THINGS. SHE LIKED THAT MOST OF ALL.

CONNEE HAD TO GET THROUGH MANY EXTENSIVE PHYSICAL AND MENTAL CHALLENGES TO GAIN ACCEPTANCE TO THE RETREAT. IN HER CURRENT PHYSICAL STATE, SHE KNEW IT WOULD BE IMPOSSIBLE TO PASS SOME OF THE TASKS. HOWEVER, SHE DECIDED SHE WOULD APPLY AND GIVE IT HER BEST.

WHEN CONNEE WENT TO THEIR MAIN OFFICE TO APPLY, SHE WAS TOLD THAT THE APPLICATION DEADLINE WAS OVER, AND THE INTERVIEWS FINISHED. THEN THE OFFICE PERSON MADE A CALL TO SOMEONE AND TOLD CONNEE THAT SHE COULD MEET THE TRAINING INSTRUCTOR FOR AN INTERVIEW.

CONNEE MET THE INSTRUCTOR AT A CAFE IN IN-SA-DONG. THEY SPOKE FOR A LONG TIME, AND HE AGREED TO ACCEPT HER AS A CANDIDATE. HE ASKED THAT SHE PUT IN AN APPLICATION AS A FORMALITY.

ENTRANCE EXAM

APPLICANTS WHO HAD PASSED THEIR INTERVIEWS WERE REQUIRED TO COME TO THE MOUNT JIRI TRAINING CENTER ON A SET DATE.

UPON ARRIVAL, THEY WERE REQUIRED TO PASS A TEST BEFORE BEING ALLOWED PAST THE GATE. AND MORE TESTS HAD TO BE PASSED BEFORE BEING ALLOWED INTO THE MAIN PRACTICE HALL.

ALL APPLICANTS PASSED WITHOUT MUCH PROBLEMS, EXCEPT FOR CONNEE. THOUGH SHE COULD READ, SHE COULD NOT MEMORIZE THE TWO PAGES LONG TRAINING CENTER DOCTRINE. IT WAS THEIR LIST OF DO'S AND DON'TS OF THE TRAINING CENTER, REQUIRING PARTICIPANTS TO RESPECT ALL LIVING THINGS AND LIVE IN HARMONY WITH THEM.

CONNEE WAS UNABLE TO MEMORIZE AND REPEAT IT BACK TO THE TESTER. HER BODY HAD RECOVERED A GREAT DEAL, AS WELL AS SOME OF HER MEMORY SYSTEM. HOWEVER, FOR SOME REASON HER MEMORY HAD GOTTEN WORSE SINCE ARRIVING AT THIS PLACE.

WHEN CONNEE FAILED TO REPEAT EVEN ONE PASSAGE AT A TIME, THE TESTER THOUGHT THAT SHE WAS PLAYING GAMES WITH HIM. HOW COULD A PERSON READ AND NOT BE ABLE TO REPEAT IT BACK?

CONNEE FACED AN IMPOSSIBLE SITUATION, BUT SHE UNDERSTOOD AND WAS WILLING TO FOLLOW THEIR RULES. SHE JUST HAD TO MEMORIZE THESE TWO PAGES IN ORDER TO PASS THIS GATE.

"PLEASE GO INSIDE. I WILL STAY HERE UNTIL I CAN MEMORIZE THIS AND WILL CALL YOU WHEN THAT HAPPENS."

"SO, YOU CAN DO IT?"

"NOT ANY TIME SOON. BUT I HAVE NO CHOICE BUT TO TRY."

THE TESTER COMMENTED THAT CONNEE LOOKED FINE AND CAPABLE, AS IF HE DOUBTED HER CONDITION. CONNEE EXPLAINED THAT SHE WAS A VERY CAPABLE PERSON BEFORE SHE GOT SICK. STILL LOOKING SKEPTICAL, HE REPLIED THAT HER CONDITION WAS NEW TO HIM. HE WOULD TALK WITH THE OTHERS ABOUT IT AND COME BACK TO CHECK IN ON HER AFTERWARDS.

CONNEE SAT AND MEDITATED, FOR THAT WAS ALL SHE COULD DO AT THAT POINT.

SOMETIME LATER.

"YOU CAN MEDITATE LIKE THAT IN YOUR CONDITION?"

THE TESTER HAD RETURNED EARLIER AND FOUND CONNEE MEDITATING, SO HE WENT BACK TO GET DINNER BEFORE RETURNING AGAIN. FINDING HER STILL IN MEDITATION, HE HAD GONE BACK FOR TEA.

NOW, WITH CONNEE STILL IN THE SAME POSITION AS BEFORE, THE TESTER COULDN'T BELIEVE THAT WITH HER CONCENTRATION AND FOCUS, SHE WAS INCAPABLE OF PASSING THE SIMPLE TEST.

CONNEE ASSURED HIM THAT SHE UNDERSTOOD HIS CONFUSION, BUT AS OF RIGHT NOW, SHE COULD NOT THE PASS THE TEST. SHE ASKED THE TESTER IF SHE COULD WAIT THERE LONGER UNTIL HER MEMORY FUNCTIONED ENOUGH TO PASS THE TEST. THE TESTER WAS VISIBLY CONFLICTED, NOT KNOWING WHETHER TO BELIEVE CONNEE. HE TOLD HER THAT HE WOULD RETURN AFTER CONSULTING WITH THE OTHERS.

YES. HOW DOES IT WORK?

I WANT YOU TO READ EACH PASSAGE THREE TIMES UNTIL IT'S ALL DONE. THEN YOU CAN SIGN THE DOCUMENT. WE WILL CONSIDER THAT THE SAME AS HAVING MEMORIZED THE PASSAGES.

THANK YOU! I CAN DO THAT!

THANK YOU!

CONNEE MADE SURE TO ALSO THANK THE ATTENDING WITNESSES. SHE HAD FINALLY MADE IT PAST THE FIRST GATE AND ON HER WAY TO THE MAIN HALL.

THOUGH IN THE FOLLOWING DAYS SHE PASSED OUT A FEW TIMES WHILE SOLVING RIDDLES, SHE SOLDIERED ON. FOR HER NEXT TEST, SHE WAS TO CIRCLE THE MOUNTAIN BEHIND THE CENTER, USING THE CENTER AS THE STARTING AND END POINT. THE SECOND TESTER EXPLAINED TO CONNEE HOW SHE SHOULD VIEW AND TREAT THE MOUNTAIN AS A LIVING ENTITY. AND THAT IT WAS PROPER TO ASK PERMISSION BEFORE ENTERING THE MOUNTAIN. THIS PUZZLED CONNEE.

DON'T YOU ALWAYS CALL OR KNOCK FIRST BEFORE ENTERING SOMEONE'S HOUSE?

YES. BUT IT'S A MOUNTAIN...

"HOW WILL I KNOW THAT I'VE BEEN ACCEPTED OR NOT?"

"YOU WILL GROW TO UNDERSTAND. YOU AND THE MOUNTAIN BOND WHEN EACH HOLDS RESPECT FOR ONE ANOTHER."

"I DON'T KNOW IF I CAN PULL THAT OFF RIGHT NOW."

"DON'T WORRY SO MUCH ABOUT THAT. THE MAIN THING IS TO HONOR AND RESPECT ALL THINGS AS IF THEY ARE YOURSELF."

"I WILL TRY IT. I'VE NEVER BEEN TAUGHT THIS WAY BEFORE."

"YOU WILL LEARN IF YOU ARE GOING TO LIVE HERE."

THE HIKE NORMALLY TOOK TWO HOURS TO COMPLETE. THE SECOND TESTER GAVE CONNEE INSTRUCTIONS ON WHY SHE WAS DOING THIS AND THINGS TO WATCH OUT FOR. THE TESTER WARNED HER THAT IT MIGHT TAKE THREE HOURS FOR A BEGINNER. HE ESTIMATED THAT SHE SHOULD BE BACK BEFORE DINNER.

PICKING UP A HALF-GALLON WATER JUG, CONNEE STARTED TO WALK. FROM THE FOOT OF THE MOUNTAIN, WITH NO ONE AROUND, SHE BOWED THREE TIMES FROM THE WAIST TO THE MOUNTAIN, ASKING FOR ITS PERMISSION TO ENTER. THOUGH THE CONCEPT OF A "LIVING" MOUNTAIN WAS DIFFICULT TO DIGEST, SHE STILL WANTED TO GIVE IT A TRY. CONNEE DIDN'T KNOW IF IT HAD GRANTED PERMISSION OR NOT, BUT SHE LOUDLY THANKED THE MOUNTAIN ANYWAY.

WHEN SHE FINALLY REACHED THE TOP OF THE MOUNTAIN, IT WAS ALREADY DARK. IN THE NIGHT SKY, CONNEE SAW ONE PARTICULARLY BRIGHT STAR THAT SEEMED TO SHINE DOWN ON HER.

CONNEE WAS PROUD THAT SHE HAD MADE IT TO THE TOP. THERE WERE NO FEARS OR WORRIES, AND IT WAS A WONDERFUL FEELING. SHE FELT INVINCIBLE. CONNEE THANKED HER INNER GUIDANCE, THE PEOPLE WHO HAD GIVEN HER THIS OPPORTUNITY, AND THE STARS ABOVE THAT WATCHED OVER HER.

WITH GRATITUDE AND PRIDE, SHE STARTED TO DESCEND THE MOUNTAIN.

CONNEE QUICKLY LEARNED HOW DIFFICULT IT WAS TO DESCEND IN THE DARK AS SHE CAREFULLY MADE HER WAY DOWN THE STEEP AND NARROW FOOT TRAIL. THE TRAIL SOMETIMES SPLIT TWO WAYS AND THEN MET AGAIN AS IT SNAKED THE SHOULDER OF THE MOUNTAIN WITH RAVINES ON EITHER SIDE. WITH ONE WRONG STEP, SHE WOULD FIND HERSELF ROLLING DOWN THE MOUNTAIN.

"I THINK I'M IN THE RIGHT PLACE. I'LL BE OKAY."

"DID I GET THAT RIGHT?"

"I'LL BE BACK AT THE CENTER IN NO TIME."

IN THE DARKNESS, CONNEE COULD HEAR THE DISTANT SOUNDS OF VOICES. CONNEE GUESSED THAT SHE WAS GETTING NEAR THE CENTER. A VOICE SHE RECOGNIZED AS ONE OF THE TESTERS SOUNDED MUCH NEARER THAN BEFORE.

"I AM HERE!"

"I'M ALMOST THERE!"

THE TESTER TOLD HER TO KEEP ON TALKING, BUT COMMANDED HER TO STAY WHERE SHE WAS. CONNEE WAS WAY OFF THE TRAIL, AND THEY HAD BEEN SEARCHING FOR HER.

THIS NEWS STUNNED CONNEE. HOW COULD SHE BE OFF THE PATH?

WITHOUT THEM LOOKING FOR HER, CONNEE WOULD HAVE CONTINUED ON SOME ANIMAL TRAIL GETTING FARTHER AWAY FROM THE CENTER. WHAT WOULD HAVE HAPPENED THEN?

CONNEE WOULD HAVE MISSED THE MEETING WITH HER TRUE NATURE WHO HAD LED HER THIS FAR.

AS SOON AS SHE REALIZED THIS, CONNEE BURST INTO TEARS.

FOLLOWING ONE FOOLISH THOUGHT, ONE FOOLISH BELIEF THAT SHE WAS ON THE CORRECT PATH, SHE COULD HAVE WOUND UP IN A TOTALLY DIFFERENT PLACE WITH DISASTROUS RESULTS.

BEING ALONE IN THIS WORLD IS NOT POSSIBLE, AS I HAD PREVIOUSLY THOUGHT. I WAS PROUD THAT I HAD REACHED THE MOUNTAIN TOP AND AS A RESULT LOST THE INNER CONNECTION.

THANK YOU FOR THE TEACHING!

CONNEE CORRECTED HER PRIDE AND ITS ACCOMPANYING THOUGHTS. THE PRIDE DIDN'T KNOW HOW TO KEEP HER IN LINE. SHE LEARNED THAT DISCONNECTING FROM HER INNER SELF WAS A DANGEROUS THING TO DO. ONCE SHE LOST THE CONNECTION, THERE WAS NO GUARANTEE WHERE SHE WOULD END UP.

ABOUT TEN PEOPLE CAME TO HER RESCUE, USING FLASHLIGHTS TO SPOT AND REACH HER. THEY FOUND HER WAY DOWN A RAVINE.

CONNEE HELD EACH PERSON'S HANDS AS SHE THANKED THEM DEEPLY. SHE REALIZED HOW FAR OFF SHE HAD BEEN ONLY AFTER SHE GOT BACK ON THE CORRECT PATH.

WHEN THEY ALL ARRIVED BACK AT THE CENTER, THE TEACHER AWAITED THEM ON THE PORCH, ALONG WITH THE REST OF THE RETREAT PEOPLE. WITH EVERY LIGHT TURNED ON, THEY ALL CHEERED WHEN THEY SAW THEM RETURN SAFELY. THIS MOVED CONNEE PROFOUNDLY.

WITH EVERYONE GATHERED IN THE COURTYARD, THE TEACHER SPOKE. HE REMINDED THEM HOW IMPORTANT IT WAS TO CARE FOR ONE ANOTHER. THAT EVERYONE AT THE CENTER MUST RECOVER THEIR TRUE HUMANITY. AND THINKING SIMPLY IN TERMS OF "I" WAS NOT THE RIGHT PATH TO THAT END. SPENDING HOURS, WEEKS, MONTHS AND YEARS PRACTICING "ME, I, AND MINE" WASN'T GOING TO TAKE THEM FAR AS PRACTITIONERS.

TO PRACTICE WAS TO DISCOVER WHAT TRUE HUMANITY WAS AND TO BE ONE WITH IT. SOME AT THE CENTER MAY BE PRACTICING TO BECOME STRONG AND POWERFUL WITH SPIRITUAL POWER. BUT THIS SHOULD NOT BE DONE WITH A "ME, I, AND MINE" ATTITUDE.

THOUGH THEY DIDN'T KNOW IT YET, EVERYONE WAS CONNECTED AS ONE. RECOVERING ONE'S TRUE NATURE SHOULD BE THE NUMBER ONE PRIORITY ON THIS JOURNEY.

EVERYONE LISTENED QUIETLY AND INTENTLY TO HIS WORDS.

WHEN ONE IS LOST, LIKE TONIGHT, EVERYONE IS LOST. WE WORRY AND SUFFER FROM LOSING A PART OF US. MAKE SURE ALL OF YOU MAKE IT HOME SAFELY. IF ONE IS LOST, IT'S YOUR RESPONSIBILITY AS A HUMAN TO GO LOOK FOR THAT INDIVIDUAL UNTIL SHE OR HE MAKES IT HOME. HELP EACH OTHER ALL MAKE THE JOURNEY HOME.

HIS WORDS MOVED CONNEE TO TEARS AND SHE THANKED HIM FROM DEEP IN HER HEART.

FINDING ROOTS

THE FIFTH RIDDLE AWAITED CONNEE. FORTUNATELY, MOST OF IT DEALT WITH MIND AND BODY ENDURANCE AND RECOVERING ONE'S HUMAN NATURE THROUGH ONE'S ROOTS. SOME APPLICANTS PASSED THE RIDDLE WITH FLYING COLORS. CONNEE, ON THE OTHER HAND, WAS DETERMINED TO GO THROUGH THIS WITH HER WHOLE BODY AND MIND. THIS WASN'T SIMPLY A TEST FOR HER. IT WAS REAL, AND SHE TOOK EACH STEP SERIOUSLY.

SHE ASKED THE THIRD TESTER IF SHE COULD LEAVE THE CENTER AND VISIT HER ANCESTRAL LANDS IN ORDER TO SOLVE THE RIDDLE. THE TESTER SHOWED CONNEE HOW IT COULD BE SOLVED FROM THE CENTER - A SHORTCUT THAT WAS STILL ACCEPTABLE FOR PASSING THE RIDDLE.

I AM NOT HERE SIMPLY FOR THE RETREAT. THE PATH TO FINDING MY ROOTS GOES THROUGH ME, AND IT'S IMPORTANT THAT I DO THIS FOR MYSELF.

THAT'S WHY I CAN'T TAKE ANY SHORT CUTS.

IT MIGHT TAKE YOU A LONG TIME.

I'VE DONE MANY SHORT CUTS IN MY LIFE. AND THOSE SHORT CUTS ALWAYS BROUGHT ME BACK TO SQUARE ONE. IF I WANT TO GET ANYWHERE, I CAN'T TAKE ANY MORE SHORT CUTS. I MUST BE HONEST WITH MYSELF AND FOLLOW THROUGH TO THE END.

HAVE IT YOUR WAY. BUT KNOW THAT YOUR WAY MAY TAKE A LONG LONG TIME, AND YOU MAY NOT GET BACK HERE TO FINISH.

DON'T WORRY. I WILL BE BACK TO FINISH. I DON'T HAVE AN OPTION.

DO WHAT YOU NEED TO DO. JUST KNOW THAT WE WON'T WAIT FOR YOU AND WILL CONSIDER YOU LOST WHEN YOU DON'T RETURN ON TIME.

SO YOU'RE NOT GOING TO LOOK FOR ME IF I DON'T RETURN ON TIME?

THAT'S CORRECT.

UNDERSTOOD.

EVERYONE WAS WONDERING WHAT HAD HAPPENED WHEN CONNEE RETURNED TO THE HALL. SHE QUIETLY SAT DOWN AND WAITED FOR THE CEREMONY TO BEGIN.

ALL EIGHT OF THEM WERE TO BE GIVEN A NEW NAME. AND CONNEE RECEIVED HERS.

SOME OF YOU MAY WONDER WHAT IT MEANS.

THE NAME EITHER REPRESENTS WHO YOU ARE, OR WHO YOU WILL BECOME.

CONNEE LOOKED AT HER NEW NAME..

LIBERATED

RED OX YEAR.

THE ORDINATION AND REGISTRATION

DURING THE ORDINATION, THE TEACHER SPOKE TO THE NEW MEMBERS.

"TODAY, YOU ALL REGISTER AS PART OF THE SUN DOH LINEAGE. THE PRACTICE WAS GIVEN TO US 10,000 YEARS AGO TO USE AS A LADDER TO HELP US REACH OUR HIGHER SELVES. WHEN YOU ACHIEVE AWARENESS THROUGH IT, YOU WILL UNDERSTAND WHAT THIS PRACTICE IS ABOUT AND WHAT IT DOES. YOU WILL SEE IT PURIFY THE MANY LAYERS OF ANIMAL HABITS AND THE ANIMAL MIND ASSOCIATED WITH THOSE HABITS.

THIS PRACTICE WILL BRING YOU MORE IN HARMONY AND IN UNITY WITH THE ENERGIES OF HEAVEN AND EARTH. AND THIS UNITY AND HARMONY WITHIN YOU WILL ACCELERATE YOUR JOURNEY'S PROGRESS AND ALLOW YOU TO TRANSCEND TO A HIGHER LEVEL. THE PURPOSE OF THIS PRACTICE IS TO RECOVER YOUR TRUE HUMAN NATURE, WHICH WILL ULTIMATELY LEAD YOU TO YOUR TRUE SELF.

YOU'VE LEARNED OUR PRACTICE IN ORDER TO STAY HEALTHY, AND YOU HOPED TO GAIN POWER AND INFLUENCE IN THE OUTSIDE WORLD WITH MINIMAL EFFORT. AND ALL THE WHILE, YOUR MIND REMAINED UNTOUCHED BY THE PRACTICE. NOW YOU'RE HERE TO GET TO THE NEXT PHASE. THIS TRAINING CENTER WILL PROVIDE BODY, MIND AND SPIRITUAL JOURNEY AS ONE. AND FOR YOU TO REACH YOUR DESTINATION, YOUR SINCERE DEDICATION, DEVOTION AND UNYIELDING DETERMINATION ARE REQUIRED.

SOME OF YOU THINK YOU ALREADY KNOW WHO YOU ARE. BELIEVE ME, YOU DON'T. AND YOU ARE HERE NOW TO FIND OUT. FIND THE REAL YOU AND KNOW WHAT YOU ARE HERE TO DO. THAT'S CALLED *JUNG-MYONG.**

TO KNOW AND FULFILL YOUR *JUNG-MYONG*, AS YOU ARE CALLED TO DO, THAT'S CALLED *COMPLETED JUNG-MYONG.*

IF YOU ARE HERE TO BUILD A CABIN, YOU WILL.
IF YOU ARE HERE TO BUILD A HOUSE, YOU WILL.
IF YOU ARE HERE TO BUILD A CASTLE, YOU WILL.
IF YOU ARE HERE TO BUILD TEN BUILDINGS, YOU WILL.
IF YOU ARE HERE TO BUILD A TOWN, YOU WILL.
IF YOU ARE HERE TO BUILD A NATION, YOU WILL.
IF YOU ARE HERE TO BUILD NOTHING, YOU WILL.

TO BE VERY, VERY CLEAR, MY TEACHING IS FOCUSED AND STRICT. I WILL GIVE YOU INSTRUCTIONS AND SHOW YOU THE MATERIALS. WHETHER YOU DECIDE TO BUILD A CABIN, A NATION, OR SIMPLY NOTHING AT ALL WITH IT, THE REST WILL BE UP TO YOU."

* ONE'S LIFE WORK

"IT IS NOT THE TEACHER'S JOB TO TELL YOU WHAT TO BUILD. MY JOB IS TO SIMPLY SHOW YOU THE WAY. YOU MUST DECIDE FOR YOURSELF WHAT IT WILL BE AND YOU YOURSELF MUST WORK TOWARDS BUILDING IT.

THERE IS NO MAGIC OR MACHINE THAT WILL DO IT ALL FOR YOU. YOU TAKE RESPONSIBILITY FOR EACH STEP. THE SIZE AND TIME OF COMPLETION WILL BE UP TO YOU. AND WHATEVER YOU BUILD, YOU WILL BE LIVING IN FOR THE REST OF THIS LIFE, AND THAT KNOWLEDGE WILL CARRY INTO YOUR NEXT LIFE."

"FIRST, IF YOU WANT TO BUILD ANYTHING, YOU NEED TO HAVE A SITE TO BUILD ON. AND YOU ARE THAT SITE.

SECOND, YOU MUST PREPARE THE GROUND BY CLEARING TRASH AND DEBRIS WITHIN YOU.

THIRD, REMOVE ALL UNWANTED ITEMS FROM YOUR SPACE, WITH NOTHING THAT CAN SHIFT AROUND IN YOU. AS YOU WORK ON THIS, YOU MAY REALIZE YOU WANT TO CHANGE THE SIZE OF THE BUILDING. YOU HAVE THE OPTION TO CHANGE IT ANYTIME.

FOURTH, MAKE SURE THAT YOUR HOUSE OR BUILDINGS PROVIDE ENOUGH AIR AND SUNSHINE TO BE FILTERED THROUGHOUT. BUILD IT NATURE FRIENDLY, SO THAT YOU ARE PART OF NATURE AND NATURE IS PART OF YOU.

FOR SOME, IT MAY ONLY TAKE A SHORT TIME. FOR OTHERS, IT MAY TAKE A LIFETIME. AND IF YOU BUILD CORRECTLY WITH THE CORRECT MINDSET, IT WILL BE GREAT NO MATTER HOW BIG OR SMALL.

DO NOT COMPARE YOUR WORK TO THAT OF ANYONE ELSE. REMEMBER THAT WE ALL HAVE DIFFERENT GOALS AND PURPOSE. IF YOU WANT YOURS TO BE LIKE SOMEONE ELSE'S, YOU WILL NEED TO REDO THE FOUNDATION TO ACCOMMODATE THE CHANGES. HOWEVER, THAT WILL NOT REALLY BE YOURS SINCE YOU ARE ONLY COPYING."

THE GREAT GRAND MASTERS' INSTRUCTIONS

CONNEE WAS ALLOWED TO MEET THE GREAT MASTER. HE THEN INTRODUCED HER TO THE LEGENDARY GREAT GRAND MASTERS WHO HAVE BEEN LIVING WELL BEYOND HUNDRED YEARS. NOT MANY EVER HAD THE CHANCE TO MEET THEM. HOWEVER, AS CONNEE DIDN'T KNOW WHO THEY WERE NOR HOW SPECIAL THIS MEETING WAS, SHE REMAINED UNMOVED BY THEIR PRESENCE.

BASED ON THEIR EVALUATION, CONNEE NEEDED TO ADJUST HER ENERGY LEVELS.

BY MUTUAL AGREEMENT, THE ADJUSTMENT WAS FACILITATED BY ONE OF THE GREAT GRAND MASTERS. HE EXPLAINED THE PROCEDURE TO CONNEE AND SHE UNDERSTOOD WITHOUT A SINGLE DOUBT.

AFTER THE ADJUSTMENTS, HER VIEW OF THINGS CHANGED, BECOMING MORE WHOLESOME AND WIDER IN RANGE.
THEY FOLLOWED WITH SEVERAL MORE INSTRUCTIONS AND ADJUSTMENTS.

DECODE THE BOOK AND THE LAST ENERGY DIAGRAM.

IN A FEW MONTHS, SOMEONE WILL GIVE YOU THE BOOKS AS A GIFT. KEEP IT UNTIL THE RIGHT TIME TO READ IT. YOU WILL KNOW WHAT THAT TIME WILL BE.

I'M SORRY. YOU HAVE THE WRONG PERSON FOR THE JOB. I THANK YOU FOR THE GIFT, BUT I REALLY WON'T BE READING THEM ANY TIME SOON, SO PLEASE DON'T WASTE THOSE BOOKS ON ME. AS A TRAVELLER, CARRYING AROUND BOOKS IS VERY DIFFICULT.

DECODE FIRST. IT'S ALL THERE. CONNECT THE DOTS AND TEACH YOUR STUDENTS WITH IT. YOU WILL KNOW WHY.

THE GREAT GRAND MASTER SHOWED HER WHAT HE WAS TALKING ABOUT. CONNEE WAS STILL SKEPTICAL OF HIS REQUEST.

DECODING? IS THAT EVEN POSSIBLE?

TIME WILL TELL.

HOWEVER, SHE HAD NO CHOICE BUT TO REMAIN SILENT. AND CONNEE COULDN'T EVEN SHARE THIS WITH ANYONE, BECAUSE NO ONE WOULD BELIEVE HER IN THE FIRST PLACE.

CONNEE THOUGHT THIS MUST BE A JOKE. SHE HAD NEITHER THE EXPERIENCE NOR THE RESOURCES TO DECODE THE MATERIALS. IT WAS IMPOSSIBLE!

WHAT CRAZY PLACE IS THIS? HOW CAN THESE GREAT GRAND MASTERS SEE ME EVEN DOING THIS? I CAN'T EVEN REMEMBER THINGS I'VE JUST READ. THIS IS ABSOLUTELY CRAZY. CLEARLY, THEY MADE A MISTAKE IN CHOOSING ME FOR THIS JOB!

A FEW MONTHS LATER, CONNEE WAS GIFTED WITH THE BOOKS.

SHE TRIED REFUSING, BUT THE PERSON LEFT THEM ANYWAY.

SOON AFTER, SHE FORGOT ALL ABOUT IT.

OPENING OF THE DRAGON'S EYES

DURING THE FALL OF RED OX YEAR, CONNEE'S AWARENSS GREW AND BECAME PRECISE. WHAT SHE SAW, FELT, AND KNEW WERE ONE, JUST AS HER MIND AND BODY WERE ONE.

ONE MORNING, WHILE OTHERS WERE PRACTICING IN THE MEDITATION ROOM, SHE WENT FOR A MOUNTAIN WALK TO HER FAVORITE RESTING SPOT. IT WAS LOCATED ONE THIRD OF THE WAY FROM THE TOP WHERE THERE WAS A HUMP ON THE SHOULDER OF THE MOUNTAIN. CONNEE FOUND IT BOTH CALMING AND COMFORTABLE.

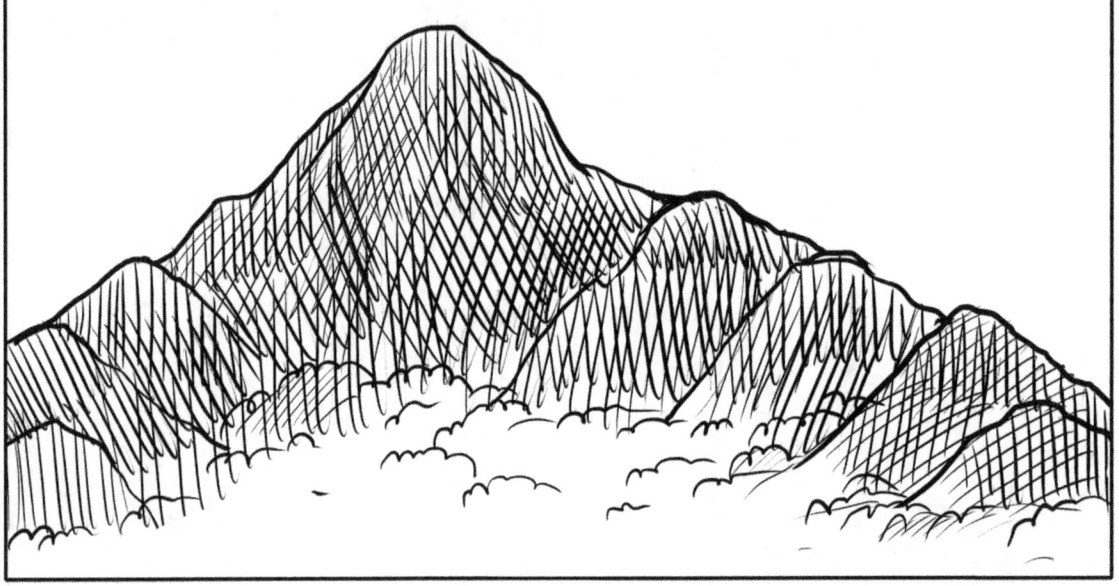

THAT PARTICULAR MORNING, SHE FELT SOMETHING MOVE BENEATH HER, ALMOST AS IF IT WAS A LIVING THING.

IT'S ONLY DIRT.

LOOKING DOWN THE DIRT SHOULDER OF THE MOUNTAIN, SHE SAW A DRAGON OPEN ONE EYE, THEN THE SECOND EYE.

UNKNOWINGLY, CONNEE HAD BEEN SITTING ON THE DRAGON'S NECK. THIS WAS COMPLETELY NEW. WITH ITS TAIL BURIED DEEP INTO THE MOUNTAIN TOP, THE DRAGON YAWNED AND STRETCHED AS IF WAKING UP FROM A LONG SLUMBER. THIS MOVEMENT WOKE EVERYTHING AROUND IT, INCLUDING A HIDDEN DOOR AT THE TOP OF THE MOUNTAIN THAT HAD BEEN PREVIOUSLY SHUT BY THE DRAGON'S TAIL.

THE SECRET DOOR OPENED TO A UNIVERSAL ENERGY PORTAL THAT CONNECTED DEEP INTO THE EARTH FROM THE MOUNTAIN TOP. IT OPENED UP A NEW WORLD.

CARRYING CONNEE ON ITS NECK, THE DRAGON FLEW TO THE CENTER OF THE ENERGY PORTAL. IT SHONE BRIGHTLY WITH THE PORTAL'S LIGHT AND WAS ONE WITH ALL THINGS. THE DRAGON DISSOLVED INTO THAT LIGHT.

THE BRIGHT SHINING LIGHT PENETRATED EVERY INCH OF CONNEE'S BODY. SHE STAYED IN SILENCE AS IT UNFOLDED, AWARE OF EVERY MILLISECOND OF THE ENTIRE EXPERIENCE.

CONNEE KNEW WHO SHE WAS WITHOUT QUESTION. SHE WAS ONE WITH THE BRIGHT LIGHT.

FOR A SPLIT SECOND, SHE THOUGHT IT WAS DONE, BUT SHE CONTINUED TO FOLLOW HER INNER GUIDANCE. THE EVENT TOOK SIX DAYS AND NIGHTS, UNINTERRUPTED. SHE WAS FULLY AWARE OF THE WHOLE EXPERIENCE, AS IT PURIFIED CONNEE'S MIND AND BODY AS ONE, PURGING DOUBT AND LEAVING ONLY THE TRUE ESSENCE.

FOLLOWING THE EVENT, CONNEE WENT INTO DEEP MEDITATION THAT LASTED FOR WEEKS. SHE HAD EMERGED FULLY CHANGED AND MORE. SHE NO LONGER NEEDED GLASSES, NOR WAS SHE DEPENDENT ON DAILY SUSTENANCE FOR HER SURVIVAL.

AND AT THE END OF HER MEDITATIONS, SHE QUIETLY GAZED INTO THE DISTANCE, SEEING THE WAY BEFORE HER. IT WAS A PATH WILD AND UNTRODDEN. FREE FROM LOGIC AND EMOTIONS, AND WITHOUT RESERVATIONS, CONNEE WOULD RELY SOLELY ON HER TRUE NATURE TO LEAD THE WAY AND COMPLETE HER WORK.

GETTING UP, CONNEE MADE HER WAY DOWN THE MOUNTAIN. SHE WAS RETURNING TO THE U.S. TO BEGIN HER NEW JOURNEY.

END OF BOOK ONE

NOTES

www.ingramcontent.com/pod-product-compliance
Lightning Source LLC
Chambersburg PA
CBHW060458010526
44118CB00018B/2463